rights in progress

A guide to the European Convention on Human Rights and the Human Rights Act

Third Edition

Les Allamby

Rights in Progress

A guide to the European Convention on Human Rights and the Human Rights Act
THIRD EDITION

ISBN 1 872299 06 7

First published December 2002
Second edition - revised and updated August 2003
Third edition – revised and updated April 2007

Law Centre (NI)
124 Donegall Street
Belfast BT1 2GY
Northern Ireland

Printed by Impression Print & Design

ACKNOWLEDGEMENTS

I would like to thank the Community Foundation (NI) who financially supported the update of the third edition through its Social Justice Advisory Fund; Brice Dickson and Maura McCallion for their helpful comments on the update; and a number of colleagues for their assistance, particularly Catherine Couvert and Anne Tannahill for proof-reading, Michael Beggs for layout and design, Hilary Dillon and Kathryn Larkin for typesetting the changes and Mary Blair for hunting down court decisions, checking the progress of cases under appeal and painstakingly collating the table of case references.

Any mistakes or omissions are of course my responsibility.

DEDICATION

For Teddy and Zak and the joy they have brought to everyone who knows them.

CONTENTS

FOREWORD TO THE THIRD EDITION

The Human Rights Act 1998 has now been in force for over six years. It was enshrined into domestic legislation in October 2000 and since then there has been a great deal of judicial decision making based on the Act. In acknowledging the contribution this legislation has made, this aptly titled publication shows how central the Act has become to human rights promotion and protection. Its enactment was a major advance. By giving effect to the European Convention on Human Rights in domestic laws, the Act heralded a shift in focus towards a rights-based approach and expressly recognised that people have legal rights which should be respected. It introduced a set of values that flow from the Universal Declaration of Human Rights, dignity, pluralism, tolerance and mutual respect, values developed over centuries and designed to protect our common humanity. The legal system and public administrations have not collapsed under the weight of unfounded human rights claims. Where reform is needed this fact has been exposed; where rights are violated redress is available. There is much more to do but, as the guide shows, we should acknowledge the progress made so far.

Rights in Progress also helps to tackle some misconceptions about the legislation. It shows how the Human Rights Act is for everyone. It protects majorities and minorities. As the Law Centre knows well, the European Convention rights are relevant in housing, planning and the welfare system. Convention principles are applicable to the health service and education system as much as the policing service and criminal justice system.

Its strength is also in showing that there is nothing to fear from the introduction of the Human Rights Act. It is a significant achievement. We should all be proud of it. Critics of the law have not fully understood its principal objectives, the contribution it has made and its potential. It has led to changes which we can all be pleased with, but we recognise that there is more work to do. Compliance with the Act is an ongoing process and the Law Centre has worked hard in partnership with others to mainstream a culture of respect for human rights in Northern Ireland. It recognises that this has to be a shared institutional responsibility and hence the value of this publication. It sets out clearly the main principles which legal advisers and those in public authority need to know if they are to explain accurately and work alongside the current legal position. The previous guides were in great demand and I have no doubt this third edition will follow that trend.

I am delighted to be associated with such an admirable piece of work, the genesis of which most appropriately originated from the Community Foundation's Social Justice Fund. I warmly commend Les Allamby, Director of Law Centre (NI), for seeing the gap which existed in this area and for moving to fill it with this excellent guide. I strongly recommend it to all those working in the field of human rights and social justice.

Monica McWilliams

Chief Commissioner
Northern Ireland Human Rights Commission

INTRODUCTION

The Human Rights Act 1998 ('the Act') came into effect on 2 October 2000 with an enormous fanfare, amidst speculation that the domestic legal landscape would be changed beyond recognition in a very short space of time. The Act is not the panacea for all legal problems, nor is it a piece of legislation that advisers can simply ignore when dealing with daily legal issues. Primarily, the European Convention on Human Rights ('the Convention') governs civil and political rights rather than economic and social rights (for example a right to social security, to housing, to a decent standard of living, to work). These rights are contained in other international human rights instruments which are not enforceable in domestic and international courts. Instead, economic and social rights are subject to governments being required to report to United Nations or Council of Europe committees on progress being made on implementing specific human rights instruments. However, in spite of the Convention containing only civil and political rights, there have been many creative examples of the Convention being used to argue economic and social rights. This is highlighted in the recent admissibility decision *Stec v UK* (2005) by the Grand Chamber of the European Court of Human Rights where it noted at paragraph 52:

> *Whilst the Convention set forth what are essentially civil and political rights, many of them have implications of a social or economic nature. The mere fact that the interpretation may extend into the sphere of social and economic rights should not be a decisive factor against such a decisive interpretation; there is no water-tight division separating the sphere from the field covered by the Convention.*

Moreover, the Bill of Rights currently being considered by the Northern Ireland Human Rights Commission may contain economic and social rights that can be enforced through the courts. Furthermore, the courts are beginning to allow arguments based on other international human rights conventions to be introduced in limited circumstances, even though such conventions have not been incorporated into domestic law. The Human Rights Act remains contentious yet, in effect, it simply provides that long-standing rights enshrined in an international treaty can be argued more readily in domestic courts rather than having to be pursued through the European Court of Human Rights in Strasbourg.

This guide aims to provide advisers and others with an introduction to using the Human Rights Act. From 2 October 2000, the Act has brought most of the provisions of the Convention into domestic law. Some parts of the Act have, in fact, been in place under the Northern Ireland Act 1998 since 2 December 1999 (when the Northern Ireland Assembly went live). As a result, the starting point is the set of rights created by the Convention. The guide begins by examining the Convention and goes on to analyse how it has been absorbed into domestic law through the Human Rights Act. The potential impacts of the Act on social security, housing, community care and other areas of social welfare law are all examined. Other case law taking into account the Human Rights Act has also been included.

Reflecting the work of the Law Centre, the guide concentrates on civil rather than criminal areas of law.

The European Convention on Human Rights and the Human Rights Act need to be seen as part of a bigger picture as human rights developments on the domestic and international stage are fast-moving. This guide is designed to provide a practical introduction to a key piece of the jigsaw by relating the Convention and the Act to the daily work of advisers and other practitioners.

Up until 1 November 1998, the enforcement of the Convention fell to the European Commission and the part-time European Court of Human Rights ('the Court') and the Commission continued to deal with cases declared admissible prior to this date up until 31 October 1999. From that date, the functions of the Commission were merged with those of the Court, which became full-time, and the Commission was abolished. For ease of reference, the term Court has been used when referring to judgments of the European Court of Human Rights and the term Commission for cases determined by the European Commission. Judgments in domestic courts are noted by emphasising whether heard by the High Court, Court of Appeal in England or Northern Ireland, Court of Session in Scotland or House of Lords. In England, the High Court is now sometimes referred to as the Administrative Court but for ease of reference the term High Court has been used.

It is worth remembering that the European Convention on Human Rights is not a product of the European Union and that the European Union's Court of Justice (in Luxembourg) is an entirely different body from the European Court of Human Rights (in Strasbourg). Finally, the Convention is a product of the Council of Europe, which has produced several of the treaties relevant to human rights (for example those covering data protection, national minorities and trafficking in human beings).

THE EUROPEAN CONVENTION ON HUMAN RIGHTS

The European Convention on Human Rights is an international treaty of the Council of Europe. It was adopted in 1950, was ratified by the United Kingdom government in 1951 and entered into effect in 1953. Unlike most other international human rights instruments, the Convention allows individuals, voluntary organisations or other social groupings to petition the European Court of Human Rights to argue that they have been the victims of a breach of one or more articles of the Convention. Since the Convention was first drafted, there has been a number of protocols added to expand the Convention. The Convention is an international legal agreement that applies to all member states of the Council of Europe, including the United Kingdom and Ireland.

Some rights contained in the Convention are absolute in that there are no circumstances in which the right can be overridden, while other rights are qualified inasmuch as the exercise of these rights is subject to limitation clauses. Article 3 (the prohibition of torture, inhuman and degrading treatment or punishment); Article 4(1) (prohibition of slavery) and Article 7 (prohibition on retrospective application of criminal law) are all examples of absolute rights. In contrast, Article 8 (the right to respect for private and family life, home and correspondence); Article 9 (freedom of thought, conscience and religion); Article 10 (freedom of expression) and Article 11 (freedom of assembly and association) are all qualified rights and are subject to limitations in specific circumstances.

To understand the Convention and how it operates in practice, it is important to understand a number of key principles that underpin its interpretation. The role of individual countries in protecting human rights is different from that played by the Court. Article 1 provides that each country applying the Convention must secure these rights to everyone within the country (save for any derogations or reservations). Article 13 sets out that each country signed up to the Convention must ensure there is an effective domestic remedy to challenge violations of that Convention. Normally, the Court will not consider any case until all domestic remedies have been exhausted. The role of the Court in reaching its decision is not to substitute its own assessment for one carried out by a domestic court. Instead, the Court examines whether the individual state has applied the Convention appropriately. The Court gives individual countries a 'margin of appreciation' (in effect, some discretion to take account of cultural traditions and values) when considering the scope of human rights contained in the Convention. The extent of the margin of appreciation afforded by the Court will depend on the context. As a general rule, a wide scope has been given to issues of national security, tax, moral questions and social and economic policy. On the other hand, a narrow margin of appreciation has been afforded in cases concerning criminalising homosexual conduct between consenting adults, freedom of speech concerning political debate or matters of public interest. The margin of appreciation does not provide a country with complete freedom in meeting its Convention obligations.

In addition, the Court will take into account whether there is a general consensus on how particular issues are dealt with across the European countries: see, for example, *Petrovic v Austria* (1998). Moreover, the Convention is interpreted as a living and evolutionary document. The Court will take into account developments in social attitudes and social provision within individual states and across signatory states as a whole. In *Goodwin v UK* (2002), a case concerning discrimination against transsexuals, the Court noted:

> *While the Court is not formally bound to follow its previous judgments, it is in the interests of legal certainty, foreseeability and equality before the law that it should not depart, without good reason, from precedents laid down in previous cases. However, since the Convention is first and foremost a system for the protection of human rights, the Court must have regard to the changing conditions within the respondent State and within Contracting States generally and respond, for example, to any evolving convergence as to the standards to be achieved. It is of crucial*

importance that the Convention is interpreted and applied in a manner which renders its rights practical and effective, not theoretical and illusory. A failure by the Court to maintain a dynamic and evolutive approach would indeed risk rendering it a bar to reform or improvement.

The Court also regularly examines the legality of any restriction on a Convention right by considering whether the restriction has a legitimate aim, corresponds to a pressing social need and is necessary and proportionate. The application of the proportionality test varies according to the type of issue under review. A strict approach is adopted when questions of freedom of expression arise: see *Sunday Times v UK (No 2)* (1979) and *Stankov and United Macedonian Organisation Ilinden v Bulgaria* (2001), or intimate private or moral matters: see *Dudgeon v UK* (1981) and *Lustig Prean and Beckett v UK* (1999). On property issues, a less rigorous test is applied, namely whether there is a reasonable relationship between the interference and legitimate aim pursued or a fair balance has been struck between the competing general community interests and individual interests at stake: see *James and others v UK* (1986) and *Hatton v UK* (2003). In all situations, the Court looks carefully at whether the restriction impairs the very essence of the right contained in the Convention. Where this occurs, the Court will often overrule a restriction applied in an individual country.

In addition, under Article 15 governments can issue derogations (ie an arrangement not to apply a part of the Convention) if there is a public emergency threatening the life of a nation. The derogation must only be to the extent strictly necessary given the circumstances and remain consistent with other obligations under international law. An original derogation contained in the Human Rights Act was revoked in February 2001. However, following the events of 11 September 2001, the UK government entered a derogation to Article 5 (1) (f) (right to liberty and security). This was designed to allow for provisions in the Anti-Terrorism, Crime and Security Act 2001 to detain indefinitely without trial for-

eign nationals whose presence in the United Kingdom was considered a risk to national security, but whose deportation would put them at risk of ill treatment. The derogation led to a challenge in *A, X and others v Secretary of State for the Home Department* (2004). The House of Lords held that the provisions of the Act involving indefinite detention of foreign nationals without trial were incompatible with the Convention. In particular, the Law Lords held that the applicants had not demonstrated strong enough grounds to displace the argument that, if there was a public emergency, the legislative response by the government was, nevertheless, disproportionate. It was also contrary to Article 14 (freedom from discrimination) in being applied only to non-UK nationals. The House of Lords quashed the derogation order. The government has enacted new anti-terror legislation, with the Prevention of Terrorism Act 2005 introducing derogating and non derogating control orders. A number of cases challenging control orders (where individuals can have their liberty and movement severely restricted because of alleged involvement in terrorism which cannot be tried in court) were recently successful in England and Wales and these decisions are now under appeal (see for example *Secretary of State for the Home Department v JJ and others,* which is now going to the House of Lords).

In addition, governments can enter reservations when ratifying the Convention where any law in force is not in conformity with the Convention. The UK has entered a reservation governing Article 2 of Protocol 1 (the right to education). This states that the right of parents to ensure education in conformity with their religious and philosophical convictions is subject to the provision of efficient instruction and training and the avoidance of unreasonable public expenditure. The reservation is also contained in Schedule 3, part 2 of the Human Rights Act.

Article 2

THE RIGHT TO LIFE

1. Everyone's right to life shall be protected by law. No one shall be deprived of his life intentionally save in the execution of a sentence of a court following his conviction of a crime for which this penalty is provided by law.

2. Deprivation of life shall not be regarded as inflicted in contravention of this article when it results from the use of force which is no more than absolutely necessary:

    (a) in defence of any person from unlawful violence;

    (b) in order to effect a lawful arrest or to prevent the escape of a person lawfully detained;

    (c) in action lawfully taken for the purpose of quelling a riot or insurrection.

Article 2 places a positive duty on governments to protect life as well as providing an exhaustive list of circumstances in which killing may be permitted. Although the death penalty is specifically provided for, this needs to be read subject to Article 1 of Protocol 6, which abolishes the death penalty and supersedes the provision in Article 2 giving a lawful exception to the death penalty.

Killings by army and police

A leading case on Article 2 is *McCann v UK* (1995) which concerned the killing of three members of the IRA by British soldiers in Gibraltar. In this case, the Court held that Article 2 is one of the fundamental provisions of the Convention as it enshrines a basic value of a democratic society. As a result, Article 2 must be strictly construed. In *McCann*, the Court made a general comment that:

> *The Court considers that the exceptions delineated in paragraph 2 indicate that this provision extends to, but is not concerned ex-*

clusively with, intentional killings. As the Commission has pointed out, the text of Article 2, read as a whole, demonstrates that paragraph 2 does not primarily define instances where it is permitted intentionally to kill an individual, but describes the situations where it is permitted to 'use force' which may result in an unintended outcome, in the deprivation of life. The use of force, however, must be no more than absolutely necessary.

In this respect, the use of the term 'absolutely necessary' in Article 2(2) indicates that a stricter and more compelling test of necessity must be employed than that normally applicable when determining whether state action is 'necessary in a democratic society' under paragraph 2 of Articles 8 to 11 of the Convention. In particular, the force must be strictly proportionate to the achievement of the aims set out in sub-paragraphs (a), (b) and (c) of Article 2 (2).

In keeping with the importance of this provision in a democratic society, the Court will, in making its assessment, subject deprivations of life to the most careful scrutiny, particularly where deliberate lethal force is used, taking into consideration not only the actions of the agents of the state who actually administer the force but also all the surrounding circumstances, including such matters as the planning and control of the actions under examination.

The Court, in *McCann v UK*, accepted that the British soldiers honestly believed (in the light of the information that they had been given) that it was necessary to shoot the suspects in order to prevent them from detonating a bomb and causing serious loss of life. Nevertheless, several factors influenced the Court in ruling that there had been a violation of Article 2. First, the authorities decided to allow the suspects to enter Gibraltar and to trail their activities there when they could have arrested them at the border. Second, they failed to consider that their intelligence assessment regarding the suspects' capacity to detonate the bomb from a great distance might be wrong. Third, the soldiers automatically used lethal force when they opened fire on the suspects.

The Court has recently reiterated its view that allegations of the breach of the right to life will be subject to the most careful scrutiny. In *Nachova and Others v Bulgaria* (2005) the Court examined the killing of two unarmed men of Roma background by Bulgarian military police. The Court outlined that it must take into account not only the actions of those who administered the force, but also all other relevant circumstances, including legal and regulatory frameworks in place and the planning and control of the actions under scrutiny. The use of lethal force by the police under Article 2 is permitted in some circumstances. However, any use of force must be no more than absolutely necessary and be strictly construed. In principle, there is no necessity to use lethal force where a suspect poses no physical threat, and is not suspected of having committed a violent offence. This applies even if the failure to use lethal force results in the suspect escaping arrest. The Court held that the deaths in this case were a violation of Article 2. The legal framework and regulations applied to arrests were deficient and planning and control of operations were flawed. The concept of proportionality was not applied in the carrying out of the arrest.

In *Bubbins v UK* (2005), the Court examined the fatal shooting of an intruder who turned out to be a lawful householder who had returned to his flat drunk and without keys. The man was shot dead after appearing to aim a gun at a police officer. The weapon was in fact a replica gun. The Court held there was no violation of Article 2 in that use of firearms by the police was regulated by law with a system of adequate and effective safeguards to prevent arbitrary use of lethal force.

In a number of Northern Ireland cases, for example *Kelly and Others v UK* (2001), *Shanaghan v UK* (2001) and *McKerr v UK* (2001) the Court has made it clear that it will not enter into a fact-finding role about the lawfulness of killings by police or soldiers. Instead the Court has examined the effective-

ness of investigation actions following such deaths.

The Court has also examined the duty of the police to protect individuals from being killed. In *Osman v UK* (1998) the complaint concerned the police's failure to take proper measures to prevent a murder taking place. The Court held that the police has a positive obligation to protect the right to life by preventing an offence against a person where there is a real and immediate risk. However, this obligation has to be interpreted in a way that does not place a disproportionate or impossible burden on the authorities. The Court went on to hold that public policy which protected the police from claims for negligence was a breach of Article 6 and the right to access to the court.

In the High Court in England and Wales in *Van Colle v Chief Constable of Hertfordshire Police* (2006), the question arose whether the police could be sued for negligence. In this case, the High Court held that there was a positive obligation in certain circumstances to take preventive operational measures to protect an individual against the risk of criminal acts of a third party. The authorities must do all that can be reasonably expected of them to avoid that risk. The judgment went on to qualify *Osman* inasmuch as the judge qualified the immediate risk as meaning the risk was present at the material time. The applicants, who were the parents of the murder victim, were awarded damages.

Investigations of deaths

In *Jordan v United Kingdom* (2001), the Court ruled that there should be an effective investigation when individuals have been killed as a result of the use of force. Such an investigation is essential in order to secure effective implementation of domestic legislation to protect the right to life. The Court held that the inquest procedures applied in Northern Ireland did not satisfy the necessary requirements. This was because of the lack of information given to victims' families, non-disclosure of witness statements and the lack of availability of legal aid for inquests. In addition, the Court was critical of the lack of independence of police officers investigating the incident from those implicated in it.

The Court set out a number of principles which should be met to ensure an effective investigation. These include that proceedings must be initiated by the state, be independent, open to a determination of responsibility with appropriate punishment where necessary, ensure sufficient public scrutiny to provide proper accountability, take place promptly and allow the next of kin to participate meaningfully. These principles have been endorsed by the House of Lords in *R (Amin) v Secretary of State for Home Department* (2003).

In *Finucane v UK* (2003), the European Court set out a number of principles regarding effective official investigations where a person has been killed by force. Such investigations must be to secure effective implementation of domestic laws which protect the right to life. In cases involving state agents or bodies, an investigation must ensure accountability for deaths occurring under the state's responsibility. The initiative for an investigation must come from the state and not be left to the initiative of family members of the deceased. An effective investigation in such circumstances must also be carried out by persons independent of those implicated by the events under scrutiny. Such independence must be hierarchical, institutional and practical. The investigation must also be effective in the sense of being capable of deciding whether the force used was justifiable in the circumstances and to enable the identification and punishment of those responsible for any criminal offence. Reasonable steps must also be taken to secure evidence about the incident, including eye-witness testimony, forensic evidence and where appropriate an autopsy providing a complete and accurate record of injury and an objective analysis of clinical findings, including the cause of death. In the specific case, the Court held that the original police investigation, inquest and failure of the Department of Public Prosecutions to give reasons for decisions not to prosecute all fell short of the standards of an effective investigation required by Article 2. The principles outlined in the Finucane case were endorsed in *Nachova and Others v Bulgaria* (2005) where the Court ruled there must be an effective official investigation of individuals killed by force. The investigation must be impartial and effective and lead to a prosecution where appropriate. The investigation in *Nachova* was held to be deficient on a number of counts.

A violation of Article 2 was also found in *McKerr v UK* (2001) and *McShane v UK* (2002), both cases emanating from Northern Ireland, where a number of flaws with the inquest procedure were again highlighted by the Court. In response to these and other judgments the government presented proposals to the Committee of Ministers of the Council of Europe to provide for an effective implementation of Article 2, though the Council has yet to express full satisfaction with the measures proposed. In the McKerr case the government decided not to carry out any further investigation into the death. As a result, the family took further legal action to secure a new coroner's inquest. The House of Lords in Re *McKerr* (2004) refused the application, holding that the Human Rights Act was not applicable to a death occurring before the Act came into force. The Court of Appeal in Northern Ireland followed this judgment in *Police Service v McCaughey and Grew* (2005), although with regard to duties of the police to provide information, the Court of Appeal noted that restrictions applied to pre-Human Rights Act cases are all unlikely to apply to deaths occurring after the Act came into effect.

The House of Lords has how given judgment on a further appeal in this case. *McCaughey v Chief Constable of Police Service* and *Jordan v Lord Chancellor and another* (2007) confirmed that the Human Rights Act cannot be applied to the investigation of the death of the applicants or the inquest where the deaths occurred before the introduction of the Human Rights Act. In *McCaughey* the House of Lords did hold that under the Coroners Act (NI) 1959 a coroner is entitled to receive such information as is in the possession of the Police Service of Northern Ireland or that the Police Service is able to obtain subject to any relevant privilege or immunity.

In *Bubbins v UK* (2005) the Court held that the inquest procedure in England and Wales met the requirements of Article 2. However, the Court held that Article 13 (the right to an effective remedy) had been violated as the applicant's family had no right to seek financial damages under civil law where a different standard of proof would apply.

The relationship between investigations into deaths and Article 2 has been explored in other settings. The Court, in *Edwards v UK* (2002), raised concerns about the procedures adopted in England when initiating a private inquiry to investigate a death in custody. In this case, a violation of Article 2 was found where a young prisoner on remand was placed in a cell with another prisoner known to be suffering from a personality disorder. The young prisoner was attacked and killed by his cellmate. The Court held that the prison authorities knew or ought to have known the danger posed by sharing a cell in these circumstances and that steps could have reasonably been taken to avoid the risk.

In contrast, no breach of Article 2 was found in *Keenan v UK* (2001) where prison authorities failed to prevent a prisoner from committing suicide. The Court held:

> *The scope of the positive obligation must be interpreted in a way which does not impose an impossible or disproportionate burden on the authorities. Not every claimed risk to life therefore can entail for the authorities a Convention requirement to take operational measures to prevent that risk from materialising.*

> *For a positive obligation to arise, it must be established that the authorities knew or ought to have known at the time of the existence of a real and immediate risk to the life of an identified individual from the criminal acts of a third party.*

In *R(D) v Secretary of State for the Home Department* (2006), the Court of Appeal in England held that investigations of attempted suicides in prison should, however, comply with Article 2. Unlike deaths in custody there is no statutory framework for investigating attempted suicides. The Court of Appeal upheld the significant detail as to the re-

quirements of an Article 2 compliant inquiry in such cases that had been set out in an earlier High Court judgement. In particular, when determining the minimum requirement needed for an effective investigation the circumstances surrounding any suicide attempt must be taken into account. In D's case the circumstances included that D was known to be a real and immediate suicide risk, the seriousness of the incident and its consequences (he suffered permanent and disabling brain damage) and issues covering whether more could have been done to deal with the risk. The inquiry should be in public (save where there are convention-compliant reasons to hear witnesses or other parts of the proceedings in private), be able to compel the attendance of witnesses, D's representatives should be given reasonable access to all relevant evidence and adequate public funding should be available to allow D's legitimate interests to be represented at the investigation. The Court of Appeal endorsed these principles save that it held it was not necessary for D's representatives to have the right to cross-examine witnesses in a public hearing in order to comply with articles 2 and 3.

A number of these principles were also set out in the High Court in Northern Ireland in *re Mongan's application* (2006) where the High Court also held that promptness was one of the elements of an effective investigation. An investigation with a satisfactory outcome may still be flawed if the conclusion is not reached with reasonable expedition.

In *Sieminska v Poland* (2001), the Court accepted that the positive obligations of the state:

> *include a requirement for hospitals to have regulations for the protection of their patients' lives and also the obligation for establishing the cause of a death which occurs in hospital and any liability on the part of the medical practitioners concerned.*

The Court also found that the lack of appropriate medical treatment in this case did amount to inhuman and degrading treatment and a breach of Article 3.

In *R(Takoushis) v Coroner for Inner North London*

(2005), the Court of Appeal laid down a number of principles arising from a death allegedly caused by medical negligence. In particular, the Court of Appeal held that the need for an effective investigation extended beyond cases where there was a potential breach of the positive obligations to protect life to those where agents of the state may bear responsibility for the loss of life. The obligation under Article 2 is to establish a framework of legal protection including an effective judicial system for determining the cause of death and any liability of the medical professionals involved in the case. This does not impose an obligation to investigate every death in which clinical negligence is alleged. The Court of Appeal went on to draw a distinction between the requirements for an effective investigation in clinical negligence and death in custody cases. In clinical negligence cases the investigation does not have to be initiated by the state (though it may include such an investigation). Allowing a family to take a civil action for negligence will not be a sufficient discharge of the state's obligation in every case. This is because litigation may not be practical and liability may not have been admitted by the medical authorities. The Takoushis ruling appears to say, in effect, that a person will not know whether there has been a sufficiently effective investigation until the reality of the investigation provided by civil litigation has been ascertained.

The Court of Session in Scotland has held in *Anderson v Scottish Ministers* (2000) that Article 2 does create a duty to consider the protection of life of the general public when deciding whether to release a mentally disordered patient from an institution.

Medical treatment and other health matters

Another area in which Article 2 has been involved has been over the question of the lawfulness of abortion. The question has arisen as to whether the right to life in Article 2 extends to the unborn child. The Court has not given a definitive ruling on this point, in part because the division the issue provokes in society is mirrored in the Court itself.

This was reinforced in the recent decision of *Tysiac*

v Poland (2007) where the Court considered Polish law on abortion. The Court noted that the law in Poland prohibited abortion but provided for certain exceptions. It held that it was not therefore the Court's task to examine whether the Convention guarantees a right to have an abortion. The Court did consider that on the facts of the particular case before it, there had been a violation of the right to respect for private life under Article 8.

In *Vo v France* (2004), the applicant had her pregnancy terminated due to an unrelated medical procedure being conducted on her as a result of mistaken identity. Action was taken unsuccessfully in the domestic courts arguing unintentional homicide by the doctor. The applicant argued that the absence of criminal legislation to punish such an offence was a violation of Article 2. The Court held there was no violation, ruling that under previous case law an unborn child could not be understood as a person protected by Article 2. Nonetheless the possibility of protection was left open in that in certain circumstances safeguards may be extended to an unborn child. In addition, the Court noted that if an unborn child had a right to life it was limited by the mother's rights and interests under Article 8. The Court declined, however, to give a definite ruling on the question of whether an unborn child was a person with a right to life under Article 2.

The question of whether Article 2 has been violated has been considered in a number of other instances. For example, in *D v UK* (1997), a person dying of Aids was due to be deported to St Kitts, where medical and social conditions would accelerate death. The Court held no violation of Article 2, but decided Article 3 (freedom from inhuman treatment or punishment) had been infringed. In *N v Secretary of State for Home Department* (2005) before the House of Lords, a Ugandan national with HIV whose life expectancy would be significantly reduced if she were deported failed in her appeal. The Court distinguished the circumstances in this case from *D v UK* and held that the difficulty in obtaining suitable treatment in Uganda was not sufficiently exceptional to satisfy the very high threshold set to constitute a breach of Article 3. An application to the Court in Strasbourg is being made in this case.

In *Association X v UK* (1978), the Court considered the question of whether a vaccination programme, which it was claimed led to the death of babies, violated the right to life. The Court rejected the argument on the facts but, nonetheless, held that the scope of the right to life goes beyond the intentional taking of life to the taking of appropriate steps to safeguard life.

The Court of Appeal in England in *NHS Trust A v M* (2001) considered whether the existing case law on withdrawal of treatment from individuals in a persistent vegetative state was in accordance with Article 2. The Court concluded that existing case law was in line with Article 2 and that there was no breach as a result of withdrawal of treatment.

In *Burke v UK* (2006), the Court considered guidance issued by the General Medical Council on the withholding and withdrawing of life-prolonging treatment. The Court held that the guidance was not contrary to Article 2, Article 3 and Article 8. The applicant, who was terminally ill, wanted to ensure he would receive nutrition and drink when close to death and unable to signify his own needs. The Court observed that UK law was in favour of prolonging treatment whenever possible. The judgment noted that where a patient could not communicate then artificial nutrition should continue as long as it prolonged life, but that in some circumstances such treatment could hasten death. In light of this it was impossible to lay down rules as to what is in the best interests of a patient. In an earlier ruling the Court of Appeal had set out at paragraph 162 that:

> *Article 2 does not entitle anyone to continue with life-prolonging treatment where to do so would expose the patient to 'inhuman or degrading treatment' breaching Article 3. On the other hand, a withdrawal of life-prolonging treatment which satisfies the exacting requirements of the common law, including a proper application for the intolerability test, and in a manner which is in all other respects compatible with the patient's rights under Article 3 and Article 8 will*

> *not, in my judgment, give rise to any breach of Article 2.*

In a high-profile case, *Pretty v UK* (2002), the Court considered whether the refusal of the prosecuting authorities to give an undertaking not to prosecute a husband if he assisted his terminally ill wife to commit suicide was contrary to Article 2. The applicant, who suffered from motor neurone disease, was unable to physically commit suicide without assistance, though she remained mentally capable and alert. The Court held that there had been no breach of Article 2 as no right to die, whether at the hands of a third party or with the assistance of another person, could be read into the Article. There was also no positive obligation on the government under Article 3 to give an undertaking not to prosecute.

Article 3

FREEDOM FROM TORTURE, INHUMAN AND DEGRADING TREATMENT OR PUNISHMENT

No-one shall be subject to torture or to inhuman or degrading treatment or punishment.

In *Ireland v UK* (1978), the Court set out that ill-treatment must reach a minimum level of severity to violate Article 3. The assessment of this minimum level is relative inasmuch as all the circumstances of the treatment must be taken into account including the duration of the treatment, its physical or mental effect and, in some cases, the sex, age and state of health of the victim. The Court defined three categories of ill-treatment:

■ **torture:** deliberate inhuman treatment causing very serious and cruel suffering;

■ **inhuman treatment:** treatment that causes intense physical and mental suffering;

■ **degrading treatment:** treatment that

arouses in the victim a feeling of fear, anguish and inferiority capable of humiliating and debasing the victim and possibly breaking his or her physical and moral resistance.

In re *Mindoukna's application* (2004), the High Court in Northern Ireland endorsed this approach, holding that ill-treatment must have a certain degree of severity relative to the circumstances including its duration, pre-meditated effect and the age, sex and health of the victim. In addition, there must be evidence to prove or infer beyond a reasonable doubt the existence of the ill-treatment where there was a credible allegation of ill-treatment at the hands of state agents. Further, there must also be an effective official investigation capable of leading to the punishment of the offender.

In *A and Others v Secretary of State for the Home Department* (2005), the House of Lords held that the common-law rule against the admission of evidence extracted by torture was absolute regardless of where the torture was inflicted. In this case, the Home Office argued that information gained from torture in other countries could be taken into account in certain circumstances. Moreover, the House of Lords ruled that the exclusion of evidence gained under torture was an essential requirement of due process and a fair trial guaranteed by Articles 5(4) and 6(1) of the Convention.

Ill-treatment of children

The issue of what constitutes torture or inhuman and degrading treatment has arisen in many different contexts. For example, the question of corporal punishment in schools and parents physically disciplining their children has given rise to a number of cases.

In *Costello Roberts v UK* (1993), the Court held by a narrow majority that a private school's beating of a child aged seven with a rubber-soled gym shoe leaving no bruising was not contrary to Article 3. The Court did hold that the government should, however, exercise a measure of control over private schools in order to safeguard the guarantees contained in the Convention. In *Campbell and Cosans v UK* (1982), the threat of corporal punishment was not sufficient to constitute degrading treatment. The Court did go on to hold that Article 2 of Protocol 1 (the right to education) had been violated as the parent's express wishes about corporal punishment not being applied or threatened had not been respected.

Legislation banning corporal punishment in all schools has now been enacted. This legislation was challenged in England and Wales by head teachers, teachers and parents of children attending an independent school. The applicants argued that the ban was contrary to their freedom of religion and education where parents wished corporal punishment to be applied. The House of Lords in re *Williamson and Others v Secretary of State for Education and Employment and others* (2005) held that the legislation barring corporal punishment in schools was valid. The House of Lords held that the Convention was engaged in that the legislation did materially interfere with parental rights. However, the interference was necessary in a democratic society in order to protect the rights and freedoms of others. The legislation pursued the legitimate aim of protecting and promoting the well-being of children and was proportionate.

In *A v UK* (1998), a complaint was lodged on behalf of a child who was repeatedly beaten by his stepfather with a stick. In the domestic court, a successful defence was made to the charge of assault occasioning actual bodily harm on the grounds that the punishment was reasonable and moderate parental chastisement. The European Court of Human Rights, however, found that the punishment met the level of severity prohibited by Article 3. The Court held that the UK government's failure to provide adequate and effective protection against corporal punishment was contrary to its obligations to secure the rights and freedoms defined in the Convention. As a result of this case, the government has recently introduced a change in the law through Article 2 of the Law Reform (Miscellaneous Provisions) (NI) Order 2006. This restricts the defence of reasonable chastisement to a charge of common assault and precludes it being used on more serious charges including cruelty to persons under sixteen and assault occasioning actual bodily harm.

In *R v H* (2001), the Court of Appeal in England considered what can now constitute a defence of reasonable chastisement in a criminal action following European Court decisions. The Court of Appeal held that a judge should direct a jury to take into account the nature and context of the accused's behaviour, the duration of the physical punishment, its physical and mental consequences in relation to the child, the age and personal characteristics of the child and the reason given for carrying out the punishment in the first place. In effect, a positive obligation is created so that children are effectively protected by law from treatment contrary to Article 3.

In *Z and Others v UK* (2001), the applicants were children in one family who had been abused and neglected by their parents. The children had been referred to the local authority social services department. Despite an extensive number of reviews, case conferences and discussions, the children were not taken into foster care for five years. Proceedings were taken against the local authority for negligence and a breach of statutory duty. The claims were struck out by the court on the ground that the law did not recognise a duty of care on local authorities to protect a child from harm. This was confirmed by the Court of Appeal and House of Lords. A claim for compensation was also lodged on behalf of the children with the Criminal Injuries Compensation Board due to severe neglect, deprivation, emotional and physical abuse. There were also signs of sexual abuse. The Board awarded some compensation, but nothing for the appalling neglect that it accepted had occurred, save where an injury had been suffered. The Court held that Article 3 had been violated, in that states are required to take measures to ensure individuals are not subjected to torture or inhuman or degrading treatment including ill-treatment from private individuals. Such measures should include providing effective protection of children and other vulnerable groups and taking reasonable steps to tackle ill-treatment where it comes to the attention of authorities. The extent of the neglect and abuse in

this case did meet the threshold of inhuman and degrading treatment under Article 3.

Medical treatment

The withdrawing of medical treatment from patients in a persistent vegetative state does not constitute inhuman and degrading treatment where it is in the patient's best interest. This conclusion was reached by the Court of Appeal in England in *NHS Trust A v M* (2001) which held that for it to be a breach the victim must be aware of the inhuman and degrading treatment.

In *R (B) v SS (Responsible Medical Officer) and Others* (2006), the Court of Appeal in England examined the question of medical treatment against the wishes of a patient. The applicant had mental health problems and had been detained in a mental hospital following his conviction for rape. In the particular case, the Court of Appeal ruled that B did not have the capacity to consent to treatment. The Court of Appeal went on to consider what should happen in cases where a patient does possess capacity to consent. The Court of Appeal held that if compulsory detention was justified to protect others from harm then it was illogical to apply a higher standard to justify the administration of treatment. In addition, the European Court of Human Rights had held that as a general rule a measure which is a therapeutic necessity cannot be regarded as inhuman or degrading providing a medical necessity has been shown to exist. In B's case this had been demonstrated alongside the fact that the treatment was in the best interests of the patient and followed mental health legislative procedures.

In *R Munjaz v Ashworth Hospital Authority (Mersey Care NHS Trust) and Others* (2005), the House of Lords held that seclusion of mental patients who had been lawfully detained within a hospital did not infringe Article 3, as, if properly implemented, the policy protected patients from treatment prohibited under Article 3. The House of Lords also rejected the argument that the practice was contrary to Articles 5 and 8 of the Convention.

Prison conditions

In *McGlinchey v United Kingdom* (2003), the applicants were family members of a woman who suffered heroin withdrawal symptoms while in prison. She was admitted to hospital and died. The inquest recorded an open verdict and the family was advised there was not enough evidence to bring proceedings for negligence. The Court held that there was a violation of Article 3 in that the quality of treatment amounted to inhuman and degrading treatment. The lack of a right to compensation was also contrary to Article 13 and non-pecuniary damages were awarded.

In *Mouisel v France* (2002), the Court also found a breach of Article 3 in the treatment of a prisoner with leukaemia. The Court held that, in view of the seriousness of the ill health, the applicant should have been moved to a hospital and placed under surveillance.

In *Price v United Kingdom* (2001), the applicant was severely disabled and was imprisoned for contempt of court. Her prison conditions were dangerously cold, risked the development of pressure sores and did not allow her to go independently to the toilet and keep herself clean. This was held to amount to degrading treatment and was contrary to Article 3. In *Khudoyorov v Russia* (2005), the Court held that the prison conditions pending trial and transport to and from court were a violation of Article 3. In particular, there was a toilet in the applicant's cell which did not flush. Further, the cell was small, infested with insects and rodents, and cell windows were covered with metal shutters blocking out natural light and fresh air. The conditions of transport to court were poor and on court days the applicant received no food and missed outdoor exercise. He was also only permitted to talk to close relatives during visits in a language they were unfamiliar with. The Court also held the length of proceedings were contrary to Articles 5(4) and 6(1) and the Court awarded non-pecuniary damages.

In *Martin v Northern Ireland Prison Service* (2006), the High Court in Northern Ireland considered whether using a pot in a cell for toileting needs and having to empty the contents in a communal area (slopping out) was contrary to Article 3. The High Court held the totality of conditions and circumstances must be looked at when considering a breach of Article 3. The prisoner occupied a cell in Magilligan on his own, could use the pot in privacy and for a significant part of the day could leave the cell to use ordinary toilet facilities. An overnight unlock system could also be utilised to gain access to toilet facilities at night, though this provision operated imperfectly. The High Court held that the sanitation arrangements were less than ideal but fell short of amounting to degrading treatment under Article 3. The judgment went on to hold that the applicant's right to a private life under Article 8 had been violated as Prison Service arrangements to minimise the impact of slopping out had not been applied consistently. The Prison Service had also not addressed its mind to the implications of Article 8 in implementing slopping out procedures.

The European Court has recently held in *Wainwright v UK* (2006) that strip-searches applied to the applicant before visiting a family member in prison did not reach the minimum level of severity to involve a violation of Article 3 even though it had caused substantial distress. The Court went on to hold that the prison authorities had not followed their own procedures in conducting the strip-search and the case was within the scope of Article 8. Although the strip-search was undertaken for the legitimate aim of fighting the drugs problem in prison, the way the strip-search was conducted was not proportionate to meeting that aim. The Court held that there had been a violation of Article 8 and awarded 6,000 euro damages.

In *R v Lichniak* (2002), the House of Lords held that mandatory life sentences for specific crimes did not amount to inhuman and degrading treatment.

Treatment of asylum seekers

In *X v Secretary of State for the Home Department* (2001), the Court of Appeal in England held that a decision to deport an asylum seeker with mental health problems to a country where the level of care was not as good was not a breach of Article 3. In

Bensaid v UK (2001) the Court held that an Algerian national being treated for schizophrenia and psychosis whose asylum claim failed on its merits could be deported because there was not a sufficient risk that removal would be contrary to the standards of Article 3. In contrast, a breach of Articles 2 and 3 was found in *R v Chief Immigration Officer ex p Njal* (2000) where an asylum seeker originally from Gambia was facing a deportation order. In this case, the applicant had provided credible medical evidence that lack of medical facilities in Gambia would reduce life expectancy and that there was a real risk of suicide occurring. In *J v Secretary of State for the Home Department* (2005) the Court of Appeal in England and Wales gave detailed guidance on the application of Articles 3 and 8 in cases involving the protection of a person at risk of committing suicide if removed to his or her country of origin. The Court of Appeal upheld an Immigration Appeal Tribunal decision not to grant asylum.

A number of important and high-profile cases concerned whether section 55 of the Nationality, Immigration and Asylum Act 2002, which denies welfare support to asylum seekers who do not claim asylum 'as soon as reasonably practicable' after arrival in the United Kingdom, amounted to a breach of Article 3. In practice, the courts have confirmed that the Convention can impose a positive obligation on the state to make welfare provision available where acts or omissions will result in inhuman or degrading treatment. In *R (Q and Others) v Secretary of State for the Home Department* (2003), the Court of Appeal in England held that failure to provide support to asylum seekers can, in principle, amount to inhuman or degrading treatment. The concept of treatment in Article 3 implied more than passivity by the government. Nonetheless, the denial of the right to work and deliberate lack of support where applicants for asylum can remain in the United Kingdom pending the outcome of any claim amounted to a positive act in violation of Article 3. The Court of Appeal went on to set a high threshold of what amounts to inhuman or degrading treatment. To breach Article 3, the treatment had to fall significantly beyond destitution and had

to verge on actual bodily injury or intense physical or mental suffering. In addition, it is not enough that there is a real risk of an applicant not receiving alternative support. It must be clear that charitable support would not be provided and that a person could not look after him or herself. The procedures operated to decide if section 55 came into effect were also held to be unfair. This decision is of considerable significance in other areas of public provision where public services are refused or withdrawn.

In *R v Secretary of State for Home Department ex p Limbuela* (2005), the House of Lords held that the Secretary of State was obliged to provide support to asylum seekers verging on destitution. In particular, the applicants did not have to show the actual onset of severe illness. The evidence established that charitable support was not available and the applicants could not fend for themselves. It was therefore presumed that severe suffering would imminently follow and that Article 3 was accordingly engaged. The judgment ruled that the threshold of suffering sufficient to engage Article 3 was met where an applicant was left with neither means nor alternative sources of support, unable to support him or herself and by deliberate action of the state was denied shelter, food and basic necessities of life.

In *Soering v UK* (1989), the European Court held that the individual has the protection of the Convention against deportation to a non-signatory state where the death penalty is still in place.

In *Chahal v UK* (1996), the Court held that deportation to India would create a violation of Article 3 given the likely risk of ill-treatment following any deportation. As there was a real risk of the applicant being subject to inhuman or degrading treatment it was irrelevant whether or not he posed a risk to national security. This case is one that has been heavily criticised by the government in bringing forward its counter-terror measures.

In *R (Ullah) v Special Adjudicator* (2004), the House of Lords considered the role of the Convention when deciding on the deportation of an individual to a country where the anticipated treatment would violate Article 3. The House of Lords held that it is necessary to show strong grounds for believing an individual, if returned, faced a real risk of being subject to torture, inhuman or degrading treatment or punishment. The Lords also discussed the threshold needed to meet Articles 2, 5, 6, 8 and 9. In the specific case the two applicants were held to have fallen far short of showing any violation under the Convention.

Article 4

FORCED OR COMPULSORY LABOUR

1. No one shall be held in slavery or servitude.

2. No one shall be required to perform forced or compulsory labour.

3. For the purposes of this Article the term 'forced or compulsory labour' shall not include:

    (a) any work required to be done in the ordinary course of detention imposed according to the provisions of Article 5 of this Convention or during conditional release from such detention;

    (b) any service of a military character or, in case of conscientious objectors where they are recognised, service extracted instead of compulsory military service;

    (c) any service extracted in case of an emergency or calamity threatening the life or well-being of the community;

    (d) any work or service which forms part of normal civic obligations.

The Court has never found a violation of Article 4, though it has made clear that forced or compulsory labour should be interpreted in line with International Labour Organisation (ILO) definitions. The ILO has defined forced or compulsory labour as

work which a person undertakes under the threat of any penalty and which the person has not undertaken voluntarily.

Article 5

THE RIGHT TO LIBERTY AND SECURITY

1. Everyone has the right to liberty and security of person. No one shall be deprived of his liberty save in the following cases and in accordance with a procedure prescribed by law:

    (a) the lawful detention of a person after conviction by a competent court;

    (b) the lawful arrest or detention of a person for non-compliance with the lawful order of a court or in order to secure the fulfilment of any obligation prescribed by law;

    (c) the lawful arrest or detention of a person effected for the purpose of bringing him before the competent legal authority on reasonable suspicion of having committed an offence or when it is reasonably considered necessary to prevent his committing an offence or fleeing after having done so;

    (d) the detention of a minor by lawful order for the purpose of educational supervision or his lawful detention for the purpose of bringing him before the competent legal authority;

    (e) the lawful detention of persons for the prevention of the spreading of infectious diseases, of persons of unsound mind, alcoholics or drug addicts or vagrants;

    (f) the lawful arrest or detention of a person to prevent his effecting an unauthorised entry into the country or of a person against whom action is being taken with a view to deportation or extradition.

2. Everyone who is arrested shall be informed promptly, in a language which he understands, of the reasons for his arrest and of any charge against him.

3. Everyone arrested or detained in accordance with the provisions of paragraph 1(c) of this article shall be brought promptly before a judge or other officer authorised by law to exercise judicial power and shall be entitled to trial within a reasonable time or to release pending trial. Release may be conditional by guarantees to appear for trial.

4. Everyone who is deprived of his liberty by arrest or detention shall be entitled to take proceedings by which the lawfulness of his detention shall be decided speedily by a court and his release ordered if the detention is not lawful.

5. Everyone who has been the victim of arrest or detention in contravention of the provisions of this article shall have an enforceable right to compensation.

Article 5 guarantees a person's right to liberty and security. It protects an individual against arbitrary deprivation of liberty. The Article sets out the particular circumstances in which this right can be curtailed and asserts that such circumstances must be prescribed in law and open to challenge, with compensation being awarded if detention proves to have been lawful. Article 5 is particularly important in the field of criminal law although this is not covered by this chapter. The government has derogated from Article 5 for the purposes of issuing derogated control orders (alongside non-derogated control orders) as part of the Prevention of Terrorism Act 2005.

Article 5 has given rise to a substantial number of challenges in the Court. The Article has been invoked in terms of police powers to arrest and detain: *Engel and Others v Netherlands No1* (1976), emergency powers allowing detention of terrorist suspects for long periods without being brought before judicial authorities; *Brogan v UK* (1988) and powers governing the compulsory holding of people with psychiatric conditions; *Winterwerp v Netherlands* (1979). Article 5 provides a positive right to liberty and security with limited exceptions. There is an overriding requirement that any deprivation of liberty is in accordance with a procedure prescribed in law and must be on grounds which can be substantively justified in law. In *Winterwerp v Netherlands* (1979), the Court held that the exceptions provided in Article 5(1)(a) to 5(1)(e) are to be narrowly construed and are an exhaustive list of the occasions in which a person may be lawfully deprived of his or her liberty. In addition, if domestic law is not satisfied then Article 5 is automatically breached.

Winterwerp concerned the detention of a person deemed mentally ill. The Court held that there must be three minimum conditions to justify detention, namely possession of reliable medical evidence of a mental disorder, a level of mental disorder sufficient to warrant compulsory confinement and that the condition must apply throughout the period of detention. The requirement of reliable medical evidence can be waived in an emergency.

Article 5 has a particular impact on mental health law. In *Ashingdane v UK* (1985), the Court held, in principle, that a person detained as a mental patient must be held in a hospital, clinic or other appropriate institution.

In *Johnson v UK* (1997), a Mental Health Review Tribunal had recommended the discharge of the applicant to an appropriate hostel for rehabilitation. No hostel place could be found. The Court held that the inability of the tribunal or authorities to enforce the recommendation was contrary to Article 5(1). In *R v Camden and Islington Health Authority ex p K* (2001), the Court of Appeal in England held that Article 5 was not breached where the authority exercised reasonable endeavours to provide the appropriate level of care in the community and, in the absence of finding such care, the patient remained in detention. In *R on the application of IH v Secretary of State for Home Department and another* (2003) the House of Lords held that a Mental Health Review Tribunal was entitled to decide that a detained patient should be discharged but the release deferred until satisfactory arrangements for treatment in the community were in place. In these circumstances, the House of Lords ruled that the tribunal could reconsider its decision and order continued detention. The House of Lords distinguished the facts in this case from those in Johnson. Moreover, they rejected an argument that the Mental Health Review Tribunal's lack of power to force the discharge of a patient was contrary to Article 5 of the Convention.

In R *(H) v Mental Health Review Tribunal North and East London Region* (2002), the Court of Appeal in England declared that some of the powers of the tribunal were incompatible with the Convention. In particular, the Court of Appeal held that placing the burden of proof on a patient to show that the grounds justifying detention no longer existed was contrary to safeguards established under Article 5 (1) and Article 5 (4). As a result, the burden of proof was reversed so that the authorities were required to prove that grounds justifying detention continue to exist, otherwise a patient will be released. In *re McB's application* (2004) the High Court in Northern Ireland considered the equivalent issue. In this case, the tribunal had responded to the judgment in England and Wales by placing the burden of proof on the trust and not the patient. In light of the tribunal's approach and the subsequent amending of legislation in Britain formally to implement the change, the judge did not feel it was necessary to make an order on the burden of proof. The judge did note that if amending legislation had not been subsequently passed then an order would have been made in favour of the applicant. This principle was also upheld by the Court in *Hutchinson Reid v UK* (2003). In this particular case, the Court also held that there had been no violation of Article 5(1) in that the facts justified detention. The Court noted that detention can be undertaken not only for purposes of medical treatment but also where a person needs to be supervised and controlled to prevent self-harm or the causing of danger to other people.

The Court has also looked at the speed of proceedings to decide on the legality of detention. In *E v Norway* (1994) the Court held that eight weeks was too long to assess the lawfulness of initial detention and four months was considered too long for a period review, see *Koendjbinarie v Netherlands* (1990).

In *HL v UK* (2004), 'the Bournewood case', the Court considered the question of the safeguards available to individuals admitted to psychiatric hospital as informal voluntary patients. The House of Lords, in a pre-Human Rights Act decision, had held that treatment of patients who lacked capacity but were compliant was lawful under mental health legislation. This ruling had been based on the common-law doctrine of necessity to justify admission and treatment. The Court, however, decided that the applicant had been deprived of his liberty in violation of Article 5. The Court noted that although in hospital on a voluntary and informal basis the applicant was under the complete control of health care professionals and not free to leave the hospital.

The Court also found an absence of procedural safeguards including no requirements to fix the exact purpose of admission, lack of time limits on treatment and care, no specific provision requiring continual assessment of any illness warranting admission and no right to nominate a representative to make submissions to the hospital. These safeguards were available to involuntary detained patients. In practice, if HL had sought to leave as a voluntary patient he would have then been detained formally under mental health legislation. As a result, the admission process applied to the applicant was contrary to Article 5(1) as it was not in accordance with a procedure prescribed by law. The Court also held that as an informal patient HL was unable to take proceedings to challenge swiftly any decision to refuse his release from hospital. The Court held this was contrary to Article 5(4) and rejected an argument that the right to judicial review satisfied the requirements of Article 5(4). The government has recently published proposals that will be introduced into a bill which will introduce safeguards into the Mental Capacity Act. This will provide additional safeguards which were implemented in April 2007.

In *MH v Secretary of State for Health and Others* (2005), the House of Lords considered a case where a young woman with severe learning disabilities was detained for treatment. After 28 days the woman could apply to a Mental Health Review Tribunal for an order to discharge her. However, before her mother could exercise this right on her behalf she was prevented from doing so by a responsible medical officer issuing a barring order. In addition, an approved social worker applied to the County Court to take on the role of the nearest relative. As a result, the only access MH and her mother had to a Mental Health Review Tribunal was through a reference by the Secretary of State. MH asked for reference by the Secretary of State and was given access to the tribunal within two months of her admission. MH challenged the fact that she had to rely on the Secretary of State's discretion to gain access to a tribunal. The House of Lords held that Article 5(4) of the Convention does not require every case of detention by reason of unsound mind to be considered by a Mental Health Review Tribunal. Instead a person detained should have a right to take proceedings. This right is protected through the reference of a case to a tribunal by the Secretary of State as the Secretary of State is under a duty to act compatibly with the Convention. Any failure to do so could lead to a challenge through judicial review.

In *Benjamin and Wilson v UK* (2002), the Court considered the powers of the Mental Health Review Tribunal in respect of reviewing continued detention of those in hospital sentenced to life imprisonment (or detained in hospital indefinitely) who argue they no longer suffer from mental disorder. The tribunal had powers to recommend release but such decisions were ultimately taken by the Home Secretary. The Court held that this was a violation of Article 5(4) in that to be independent of the parties in such cases the Tribunal must have the power to order release if continuing detention is held to be unlawful.

In the matter of *DE and JE v Surrey County Council*

(2006) the High Court in England considered a dispute over the transfer of DE from one residential care home to another. JE, the wife of DE, wished to have her husband transferred to the family home while the Council disputed this was in DE's best interests. The applicants sought a number of declarations against the Council, including unlawful detention under Article 5 and violation of the couple's right to respect for private and family life.

The High Court in its judgment set out a valuable summary of the principles that have emerged from case law when considering such cases. On the basis of these principles, the High Court held that in spite of the Council's claims that DE was free to leave residential care at any time, the reality was that DE was under the complete control of the Council and that had been the understanding of both DE and JE. As a result, DE had been unlawfully deprived of his liberty by the misrepresentations made by the Council about his legal position.

Other cases

In *Giles v (as the application of) Parole Board and Another* (2003) the House of Lords held that a prisoner serving an extended sentence in order to protect the public from serious harm had no right to an oral hearing before the Parole Board under Article 5(4) of the Convention once the punitive period of the sentence had been served. In *Roberts v Parole Board* (2005) the House of Lords held by a majority that the Board had a right to adopt a special advocate procedure in the parole process. Under these provisions, the Home Secretary could submit material which neither a prisoner nor a legal representative could see; instead a special legal advocate is appointed to assist the Parole Board. The House of Lords ruled this procedure did not breach Article 5(4) of the Convention.

In *R (Saadi) v Secretary of State for the Home Department and Others* (2002), the House of Lords considered the issue of whether the detention of asylum seekers in Oakington reception centre was contrary to Article 5(1)(f). The case turned, in large measure, on the interpretation of the phrase 'effecting an authorised entry into the country'. The

House of Lords held that entry remains unauthorised until the government has authorised such entry. As a result, the power to detain, providing it is proportionately exercised, does not violate Article 5. In the particular cases under consideration, the House of Lords held that the decisions to detain and arrangements made at Oakington were proportionate and reasonable.

This case was appealed to the European Court of Human Rights. In *Saadi v UK* (2006), the Court held that there had been no violation of Article 5(1), in that detention was part of a genuine process to determine whether an individual had lawfully entered the country. The detention lasted seven days which was not considered excessive by the Court. However, the Court went on to hold the failure to inform the applicant's representative for 76 hours that detention had occurred was incompatible with the requirement that reasons for detention be given promptly. In effect, this decision grants the government a broader discretion to detain potential immigrants or asylum seekers than is the care for other interferences with the right to liberty. The case is now before the Grand Chamber of the Court.

Article 6

THE RIGHT TO A FAIR HEARING

1. In the determination of his civil rights and obligations or of any criminal charge against him, everyone is entitled to a fair and public hearing within a reasonable time by an independent and impartial tribunal established by law. Judgment shall be pronounced publicly but the press and the public may be excluded from all or part of the trial in the interests of morals, public order or national security in a democratic society where the interests of juveniles or the protection of the private life of the parties so require, or to the extent strictly necessary in the opinion of the court in circumstances where publicity would prejudice the interests of justice.

2. Everyone charged with a criminal offence shall be presumed innocent until proved guilty according to law.

3. Everyone charged with a criminal offence has the following minimum rights:

    (a) to be informed promptly in a language which he understands and in detail of the nature and cause of the application against him;

    (b) to have adequate time and facilities for the preparation of his defence;

    (c) to defend himself in person or through legal assistance of his own choosing or, if he has not sufficient means to pay for legal assistance, to be given it free when the interests of justice so require;

    (d) to examine or have examined witnesses against him and to obtain the attendance of witnesses under the same conditions as witnesses against him;

    (e) to have the free assistance of an interpreter if he cannot understand or speak the language used in court.

Article 6 aims to provide a guarantee to a fair hearing in civil and criminal proceedings. The safeguards provided in criminal trials are greater than those given to civil proceedings, reflecting that the outcome at stake in criminal cases is normally more serious. This Article contains a number of safeguards and is one of the most important parts of the Convention for advisers.

What is covered?

A person must be exercising his or her civil rights in order to obtain the protection of Article 6. The Court in its case law has not established clear and absolute guidelines as to what constitutes civil rights for the purpose of Article 6. Nonetheless, some conclusions can be drawn. In *Feldbrugge v Netherlands* (1986), the Court held that Dutch sickness benefit was a civil right as individuals funded this and other benefits through deductions from pay. In *Schuler-Zgraggen v Switzerland* (1993) and *Salesi v Italy* (1993), the Court held that a civil right extends beyond social insurance schemes to general welfare assistance.

This suggests that Article 6 would apply to social security appeals. In *Smyth* (2001), the High Court in Northern Ireland held that an appeal tribunal hearing an appeal against a decision not to award Incapacity Benefit is covered by Article 6. The Court, however, ruled that a reduction in entitlement to Income Support of 20 per cent of an adult personal allowance, only recoverable if the appeal were successful, was not a breach of Article 6. The reduction of benefit, whilst discouraging the making of appeals, was held to be a proportionate means of discouraging frivolous appeals and was a legitimate policy aim which did not destroy the essence of the right to appeal. Cases have also held that a civil right includes: decisions concerning children, for example paternity custody and contact in *Olsson v Sweden* (1988); the right to practise a profession in *H v Belgium* (1987); the right to recover monies overpaid in tax in *National and Provincial Building Society and Others v UK* (1997) (though disputes about tax liabilities and assessments fall outside Article 6); and the right to planning permission in *Bryan v UK* (1995).

In *Department for Social Development v MacGeagh and MacGeagh* (2005), the Court of Appeal in Northern Ireland held that one parent could not in her or his own right apply for a departure direction against an absent parent to change the assessment for maintenance payable under the Child Support scheme. In this case, the absent parent argued that his former partner might have been involved in fraud in making her claim for Working Families Tax Credit. The Court of Appeal held that this substantive right to take legal action to determine maintenance had been ceded to the Department through the Child Support scheme administered by the Child Support Agency and Article 6 rights were not engaged in this case. In *R (Kehoe) v Secretary of State for Work and Pensions* (2005), the House of Lords decided that the right to enforce a claim for child maintenance against an absent parent lay with the Child Support Agency

and not the parent with care of the child. Article 6 was not engaged as it was concerned with safeguarding rights not according rights.

In *DD's application* (2006) the High Court in Northern Ireland considered whether the right to a statement on the need for special educational provision under the Education (NI) Order 1996 was a civil right. The High Court noted that the duty imposed on an Education and Library Board was wide ranging and provided the decision-maker with a huge degree of discretion as to the extent and way in which needs should be met and resources deployed. As such, the right was not a civil right for the purposes of Article 6.

In re *Sinn Fein's application* (2005), the High Court held that the Secretary of State's decision to withhold statutory financial assistance from Sinn Fein following the publication of a report from the International Monitoring Commission was not within the scope of Article 6. The dispute concerned arrangements for the exercise of political rights and as a result was not a civil matter covered by Article 6.

The right to a fair hearing covers all parts of the process, including what happens prior to and after the hearing itself: for example an unreasonable delay in giving a judgment or implementing a tribunal or court decision may be a violation of Article 6.

Fair hearing and delays

The rights contained in Article 6 include the right to a public hearing which, in effect, means an oral or personal hearing unless there are exceptional circumstances to justify dispensing with this right: see *Fischer v Austria* (1995) and *Jacobsson (Allan) v Sweden (No2)* (1998). The Court has been flexible in allowing parties to agree actually or implicitly to waive the right to a public hearing: see *Hakansson and Sturesson v Sweden* (1990) and *H v Belgium* (1987). Where an original hearing is held in public, the Court has been willing to allow an appeal, restricted to points of law only to be held in private, as in *Helmers v Sweden* (1991). However, where an appeal decides both questions of fact and law, then the further appeal should be in public: see *Ekbatani v Sweden* (1988).

Any hearing must be held within a reasonable time. No absolute time limit has been set. Instead, all the circumstances of the case must be taken into account including, in particular, the complexity of the case, the conduct of the parties and what is at stake for the applicant. In *X v France* (1992), two years was considered too long where a person was seeking compensation for contracting the HIV virus from an infected blood transfusion. The Court held that the domestic court should have expedited the hearing, taking into account the health and life expectancy of the applicant. In *Neves e Silva v Portugal* (1989), a delay of six and a half years to deal with a relatively straightforward civil dispute was excessive, and in *Union Alimentaria Sanders v Spain* (1989), five years to deal with a debt recovery case was held to be too long. In contrast, in *Vernillo v France* (1991), the Court held that a seven and a half year delay in dealing with civil proceedings was not excessive where the applicant was culpable for prolonging the legal action. In *Süssman v Germany* (1996), a three and a half year delay in dealing with a constitutional legal action was held to be reasonable due to special factors affecting constitutional legal actions. More recently, in *Obasa v UK* (2003), the Court held that a violation had occurred where employment tribunal proceedings took over seven years to complete. Similar violations were found in *Mitchell and Holloway v UK* (2002), where over nine years were taken to deal with civil proceedings for breach of contract and enforcement of a judgement debt, and in *Jordan (Stephen) (No2) v UK* (2002), where court-martial proceedings lasted four years and seven months. In a criminal case, *Mellors v UK* (2003), the Court held that eight months from arrest to conviction on a charge of rape was reasonable, but that appeal proceedings which lasted just over three years were an unreasonable delay and violation of Article 6. In *Kunic v Croatia* (2006) the court held that the enforcement of a judgement must be regarded as an integral part of the proceedings and was a part of the hearing.

The Court has held that particular diligence must be paid to proceedings affecting parental access to a child, employment matters, the title to land and entitlement to a disability pension.

Independence and impartiality

Tribunals and courts must be independent and impartial. The Court will look at the way members of such bodies are appointed, the duration of any term in office and guarantees of immunity from outside pressure. Such bodies must not be bound by advice given by the government. In *Findlay v UK* (1997), military court-martial hearings were held to violate Article 6(1) for this reason. As a result, a number of changes were made to court-martial hearings. In *Morris v UK* (2002), the Court held that some aspects of the court-martial system remained contrary to Article 6(1). In *Grieves v UK* (2003) the Court held that the Naval Court Martial system was contrary to Article 6. In contrast, the Grand Chamber found no violation of Article 6 in the RAF Court Martial system. The main difference was the presence of a civilian judge advocate, a permanent President of the tribunal and adequate safeguards to prevent outside pressure being exerted on members of the tribunal. Decisions of the Court have been crucial in bringing forward reform of the court-martial system.

In *Ezeh and Connors v UK* (2002), the Court held that prison disciplinary proceedings before a prison governor were a breach of Article 6(3). The nature of the charges and severity of the penalty, which included additional detention in prison, amounted to criminal proceedings. The lack of a right to legal representation in the proceedings violated Article 6(3)(c). The decision did not go on to decide whether the interests of justice required free legal assistance. As a result of this decision, serious prison disciplinary offences are dealt with by an independent adjudicator rather than a prison governor. A similar decision was reached by the Court in *Whitfield and Others v UK* (2005). This decision also found a breach of Article 6(1) in that the old type of disciplinary proceedings lacked structural independence and impartiality. In *re Graham's application* (2005), the High Court in Northern Ireland held that Article 6 was not engaged where the punishment related to a loss of privileges rather than an extension of custody in prison.

In R (*Bewry*) *v Norwich City Council* (2001), the

High Court in England held that Housing Benefit Review Boards failed the test of independence and impartiality, as local authority councillors who decided appeals stood to be affected by the outcome as a result of Housing Benefit subsidy arrangements. The government saw this challenge coming and had already transferred Housing Benefit appeals to social security appeal tribunals.

In *R (Alconbury Developments Ltd) v Secretary of State for Environment, Transport and Regions* (2001), the House of Lords considered whether the planning procedures and inquiries were compatible with Article 6. The House of Lords held that the administrative decision-making procedures were not independent and impartial given the Secretary of State's interest in the policy implications of individual decisions. However, the right to judicial review to challenge the fairness and legality of any decision was sufficient to remedy the breach. As a result, the procedures were compatible with Article 6.

In *Begum v London Borough of Tower Hamlets* (2003), the House of Lords considered the question of whether a local authority administrative review procedure on allocation of housing was in breach of Article 6. The House of Lords held that such administrative reviews were covered by Article 6 and that a review carried out by a different local authority officer was not independent and impartial. Nonetheless, the right of further appeal to the County Court remedied this defect and as a result there was no breach of Article 6.

When assessing the issue of impartiality, the courts have considered both subjective and objective tests. As a result, an applicant does not have to show actual bias, but facts or circumstances which raise a doubt as to the judge's or other decision-maker's impartiality.

In *Tsfayo v UK* (2006), the Court considered whether judicial review proceedings were sufficient to correct the lack of independence in Housing Benefit Review Board proceedings conducted by a local authority. The Court held there had been a violation of Article 6 in spite of access to judicial review, as the review board was deciding a straightforward question of fact, namely whether the applicant had good cause for delay in making a claim. The High Court on judicial review could not re-hear evidence or substitute its own views on the applicant's credibility. As a result, the High Court could not determine the central issue before the Review Board. The Court noted that this made the case significantly different from Begum and Alconbury, where the decision required a measure of professional knowledge or experience and the exercise of discretion having regard to wider policy aims. In practice, whether judicial review or other rights of appeal to courts will be sufficient to correct an earlier Article 6 deficiency will depend on the powers provided to the Court and the extent of the lack of independence in the first decision-making body.

Access to the courts

The right to a fair hearing has been broadly interpreted by the courts and includes the actual right of legal redress in the first place. In *Wilson and Others v Secretary of State for Trade and Industry* (2003), the House of Lords held that the restriction on a creditor's right to enforce a credit agreement, in that all the statutorily prescribed terms had to be signed by a debtor, did not interfere with the creditor's right to access the court under Article 6. The inability of a court to make an enforcement order was a limitation on the substantive scope of a creditor's rights but did not interfere with procedural fairness rights guaranteed by Article 6.

The European Court of Human Rights has opened up to a limited extent the right to sue certain public authorities for negligence. In *Osman v UK* (1998), the Court held that immunity of the police from civil action for negligence in failing to protect potential victims of crime was held to be contrary to Article 6. However, in *Z v UK* (2001), the Court held that the striking out of a claim as a matter of law without hearing the facts of the case was not a violation of Article 6. The Court's reasoning was that the House of Lords decision was made on grounds that a local authority social services department could not be sued for negligence, however foreseeable the neglect or unreasonable the local authority's behaviour. This approach did not amount to a procedural bar that restricted access to the courts. Instead, the domestic court was applying substantive law principles in deciding whether or not to create a new category of negligence in respect of local authority responsibilities. It was not a matter for the Court to decide on appropriate content of domestic law. The Court went on to acknowledge that the children had no effective remedy and held that a breach under Article 13 had occurred. The Human Rights Act now provides some remedy in domestic courts through section 6 and section 8.

The decision in *Z v UK* (2001) has, nonetheless, significantly muddied the waters once again as to the extent of the duty of care owed by public authorities where immunity from negligence actions is argued on policy grounds. In *JD v East Berkshire Community Health NHS Trust and others* (2005) the House of Lords considered the duty of care owed by doctors to parents wrongly suspected of abusing their children. In an earlier hearing the Court of Appeal had held that children wrongly diagnosed as abused could take legal action for compensation for negligence against doctors and social workers. This ruling was accepted and not contested at the House of Lords. With regard to the parents' right the House of Lords held that the claims were not made under the Human Rights Act but were claims in negligence. A duty of care to parents wrongly suspected of child abuse could not be created, as to do so would undermine the protection of children which is based on social workers and doctors having a sole duty to safeguard the welfare of a child. As a result, the parents could not take legal action against social workers for wrongly diagnosing child abuse against their children. This issue is likely to end up before the European Court of Human Rights again. It is debatable whether the Court would take the same line as the House of Lords, as in *TP and KM v UK* (2001) the European Court held that an incompetent child abuse investigation *could* result in a breach of the parents' rights under Article 8.

In *Fayed v UK* (1994), the applicant wanted to bring defamation proceedings following a government inspector's report into the purchase of Harrods undertaken under the Companies Act. The applicant had been heavily criticised in the report. The court action would have been met with a defence of qualified privilege preventing a successful outcome for the applicant. The Court held that the function of the inspectors was investigative and not determinative of a civil right. A government may legally impose restrictions on the right of access to court if the restrictions have a legitimate aim, are proportionate in the circumstances and do not operate to undermine the very essence of the right of access to a court. In this case the restriction was considered proportionate.

Access to legal aid

The failure to provide legal aid to allow a woman to bring proceedings for separation from her husband was held to be contrary to Article 6 in *Airey v Ireland* (1979). The test applied by the Court was that it was essential that the applicant be represented given the importance of the issue at stake and the complexity of the matters before the court. Without legal aid (and a lawyer), the applicant's access to court was effectively rendered ineffective.

The test in *Airey* was endorsed by the High Court in Northern Ireland in re DD's application (2006) where it was held that Article 6 was not infringed by a decision not to provide legal aid for representation before a Special Educational Needs tribunal under provisions allowing the Lord Chancellor to direct exceptional funding for representation in specific cases.

In *R (Jarrett) v Legal Services Commission* (2001), the High Court in England held that guidance issued under the Access to Justice Act 1999 was unlawful to the extent that it failed to provide for discretion to grant legal aid where failure to do so would make assertion of a civil claim practically impossible or lead to clear unfairness in proceedings. However, the Court has also held that governments may legitimately attach a merits test and means test to legal aid, providing they are not arbitrarily applied. The Commission has also held in *Winer v UK* (1984) and *Munro v UK* (1987), that a complete exclusion of defamation from legal aid is justifiable. A similar view was taken by the High Court in Northern Ireland in *Re Lynch's* application (2002). In *McVicar v UK* (2002), the failure to provide legal aid to allow a journalist to defend himself in an action for defamation was held not to be contrary to Article 6 as the applicant was well educated and capable of forming articulate and cogent arguments. As a result, the law was not so complex as to require a person in the applicant's circumstances to obtain assistance through legal aid. In *Steel and Morris v UK* (2005), the Court examined the failure to award legal aid to the applicants when defending proceedings brought by McDonalds for damages for libel. The Court held there was a breach of Article 6. The Court said that whether legal aid was necessary for a fair hearing had to be determined on the facts and circumstances of the case, the importance of the issue at stake for the applicants, the complexity of the law and procedure and the capacity of the applicants to effectively represent themselves. Given the complexity and the financial consequences of losing the case the denial of legal aid in this case had deprived the applicants of the opportunity to present their defence effectively.

It is clear from case law that the circumstances of any claim, the ability of the individual to present his or her own case and whether the applicant is pursuing or defending a libel action will all be important factors when dealing with such cases. Access to legal aid is likely to be an issue which will continue to raise arguments under Article 6. The question as to whether the lack of legal aid for industrial and fair employment tribunals is a breach of Article 6 remains to be tested.

Other issues

Article 6 also ensures that all parties should have a reasonable opportunity to present a case, to comment on all the evidence provided before a court or tribunal, to call witnesses, to reply to written submissions and to receive reasons for the court's or tribunal's findings. In *Hooper v UK* (2004) the Court upheld a complaint for a breach of Articles 6(1) and 6(3) where a magistrate issued an order to keep the peace without giving the applicant or his representa-

tive a chance to make submissions. The applicant was committed to custody for fourteen days. An appeal to the High Court against the procedural irregularity had already been upheld. However, the Court continued to deal with the case as there was no provision to obtain compensation unless the magistrate could be shown to have acted in bad faith.

In *SC v UK* (2004), the Court held that a child aged eleven with limited intellectual capacity must be able to participate effectively in criminal proceedings. Where there was a risk of a child not being able to participate fully then it is essential that a child should be tried in a special tribunal which can take into account a child's difficulties and make the appropriate adjustments.

In *Mousaka Incorporated v Golden Seagull Maritime Inc* (2001), the High Court in England stated that the extent of the Article 6 duty to give reasons will vary according to the nature of the decision and circumstances of the case. Nonetheless, an applicant should know why an appeal has succeeded or failed and full reasons should be given on the merits of a case, even though it is unnecessary to provide a detailed answer to every argument.

Article 7

RETROSPECTIVE CRIMINAL LAW

1. No one shall be held guilty of any criminal offence on account of any act or omission which did not constitute a criminal offence under national or international law at the time when it was committed. Nor shall a heavier penalty be imposed than the one that was applicable at the time the criminal offence was committed.

2. This article shall not prejudice the trial and punishment of any person for any act or omission which, at the time when it was committed, was criminal according to the general

principles of law recognised by civilised nations.

Article 7 prohibits the creation of new criminal offences which have retrospective application and also prevents the retrospective application of increased sentencing powers. The extension of existing offences to cover facts which previously did not constitute a criminal offence is also prohibited.

In R (*Uttley) v Secretary of State for the Home Department* (2003), the Court of Appeal in England and Wales issued a ruling that sections of the Criminal Justice Act 1991 were incompatible with Article 7. In this case Uttley had been convicted of a rape which took place before the Criminal Justice Act came into force. Under the new legislation, release after serving two thirds of a sentence was accompanied by the imposition of statutory licence conditions. Under the old legislation no such licence arrangements applied. The Court of Appeal held this was a heavier penalty and incompatible with Article 7.

In *Harman v UK* (1984), the applicant was convicted of contempt of court for having allowed a journalist to read documents, the contents of which had been read out in court. She complained that, until the ruling of the domestic court in her case, it was not an offence to show journalists such documents. The complaint therefore related either to a change in the law being applied retrospectively, or to the law being so imprecise that it was not possible to know whether a particular course of conduct was or was not prohibited. A friendly settlement of the complaint was effected after it had been ruled admissible.

In *SW and CR v UK* (1996), the applicants, who were convicted of raping their wives, complained that their convictions and sentences constituted retrospective punishment in breach of Article 7. When the offences were committed, under English common law there existed a marital exemption from rape. The Court held that there had been no violation of the Convention. It noted that Article 7 allowed for the gradual clarification of the rules of criminal liability through judicial interpretation. At

the time the offences were committed, English law had evolved to the point that judicial disapproval of the marital exemption of rape had become a reasonably foreseeable development of the law. The Court ruled in particular that 'the abandonment of the exemption was in keeping with a civilised concept of marriage and with the fundamental objectives of the Convention, the very essence of which is respect for human dignity and human freedom'.

No violation of Article 7 was found by the Commission in *Hogben v UK* (1985) when, due to a change in government policy, a prisoner serving a life sentence had his assurance of parole countermanded. Further, in *X v Austria* (1981) the Court held that a system where the length of sentence depends on the defendant's age at the time of conviction (rather than at the time the offence is committed) does not violate Article 7, provided the system was in operation at the time of the offence.

Article 7(1) also provides that there shall not be imposed '*a heavier penalty . . . . than the one that was applicable at the time the criminal offence was committed*'.

Article 8

THE RIGHT TO PRIVACY AND FAMILY LIFE, HOME AND CORRESPONDENCE

1. Everyone has the right to respect for his private and family life, his home and his correspondence.

2. There shall be no interference by a public authority with the exercise of this right except such as is in accordance with the law and is necessary in a democratic society in the interests of national security, public safety or the economic well-being of the country, for the prevention of disorder or crime, for the protection of health or morals, or for the protection of the rights and freedoms of others.

Article 8 is a key part of the Convention for advisers. This Article has evolved as societal attitudes to personal and moral issues have changed and has regularly given rise to legal issues under the Human Rights Act. The Article is also wide-ranging, encompassing respect for private and family life, the home and correspondence. Article 8 is also an example of a qualified right inasmuch as Article 8(2) circumscribes the rights contained in Article 8(1).

Family life - who is covered

Family life has been held by the Court in *GHB v UK* (2000) to go further than protecting parents and children; it also embraces grandparents and grandchildren. Beyond this, it is a question of fact and degree requiring evidence of close and genuine family ties. Foster parents, step-parents, adoptive relationships and cohabitees have been held to constitute family relationships in certain circumstances. However, in *Shackell v UK* (1999), the Court held that failure to provide widow's benefits for an unmarried couple where one partner had died was not contrary to Article 8 and Article 14 (freedom from discrimination) on the grounds that bolstering marriage as an institution was within a government's margin of appreciation in developing public policy.

The Court has rather surprisingly not normally been prepared to include long-term gay relationships as falling within the scope of family life. This was confirmed once again in the case of *Mata Estevez v Spain* (2001), where the applicant lived with his same-sex partner for ten years until his partner died in an accident. The applicant applied for a surviving spouse's pension which, under Spanish law at that time, was only payable to heterosexual couples. The applicant argued this was contrary to respect for family life. The Court held that long-term gay relationships do not fall within the scope of family life. In spite of the tendency for greater recognition of the equality of rights for gay couples in a number of European states, the Court noted there is still little common ground across all signatory states. Issues around the treatment of gay relationships within legislation is often dealt with under the right to private life within Article 8.

Family and childcare proceedings

Courts both domestically and in Strasbourg have taken a strong line in insisting the Article 8 considerations must be properly taken into account when making important decisions on the future well-being of children.

When dealing with family matters, the Court of Appeal in Northern Ireland held in re *Jennifer Connor* (2004) that a health and social services trust must conduct an exercise to assess whether Article 8 is engaged and, if so, whether any interference with a Convention right is justified. In Jennifer Connor the applicant was prevented from living with her husband as a result of a guardianship order. The parties agreed that there was an interference with family life but the question arose as to whether it was justified. The trust argued it had in effect conducted an assessment of what was in the best interests of the applicant. The Court of Appeal rejected this argument, ruling that examining whether a Convention right has been interfered with, and if so if the interference is justified, are different and distinct exercises. The failure to conduct an analysis of Convention rights will only be acceptable where in any event no other outcome than the course decided on could have been contemplated. This case must now be read in light of *Begum v Governors of Denbigh High School* (2006) where the House of Lords held that it is the substantive outcome of a decision and its compatibility with Convention rights which must be examined rather that the procedural question of whether Convention rights were formally considered when reaching the decision. In *AR v Homefirst Community Trust* (2005) the Court of Appeal found the trust had failed to have regard to a mother's rights under Article 8 in making a care order but, in the circumstances of the case, it did not reverse the lower court's decision.

In the matter of *JM (Care Order)* (2005), a trust applied for a care order for a four-year-old child. The High Court in Northern Ireland noted that any measures taken by the state which interfere with the mutual enjoyment of a parent and child's company interfere with family life. As a result, the trust must therefore demonstrate that intervention is proportionate and necessary to achieve a legitimate aim. The High Court noted in its judgement that European Court of Human Rights decisions have emphasised that there must be a pressing social need to justify the relevant interference. Such interference must be motivated by an overriding requirement to meet the child's best interests. The approach creates an obligation on the state to promote reunification of a parent and child. In this case, the justification was made out and the care plan was approved.

In *W and M (freeing from an Adoption Order)* (2005), the High Court in Northern Ireland refused a trust's application for an order allowing two children to be adopted as the trust had breached both statutory regulations and the parents' Article 8 rights. The High Court noted that freeing a child for adoption was one of the most draconian remedies known to the law and must never be entertained lightly. In this case, the parents had not been involved or consulted at a pivotal point. The High Court held that all health and social services trusts must become aware that the Convention has a fundamental impact on decisions of this nature.

In family proceedings, the Court has held in *O v UK* (1987) that parents must be properly involved in decision making, taking full account of their wishes and views. Furthermore, the right of a parent to live with or have contact with a child must be subject to a fair hearing before a tribunal or court. A parent will normally be entitled to a right of contact with his or her children unless very serious grounds exist to override this right. *In the matter of T* (2004) the High Court in Northern Ireland granted a declaration to a health and social services trust not to inform the father of a child's existence and to place the child for adoption. In this case, the father had been aware of the pregnancy, made no enquiries about the welfare of the mother and there was no possibility of a relationship commencing or any application being made in respect of the child. There was a risk to the mother due to the father's violent past. As a result, no family life was deemed to exist under Article 8.

The justification for interfering with family proceedings has been clarified in recent Court decisions. In *Elsholz v Germany* (2000), the Court held that a decision to deny a father access to his son on the grounds that contact would be harmful was unjustifiable in the absence of psychological evidence which had not been obtained. Where evidence is obtained, then it must be disclosed promptly: see *TP and KM v United Kingdom* (2000). In *Sahin v Germany* (2003) and *Sommerfield v Germany* (2003), the Grand Chamber of the Court considered decisions to deny unmarried fathers access to their children following the breakdown of their relationships. The Court held that the domestic court procedures were reasonable and provided adequate safeguards. The question whether a court should hear in person from a child involved in a custody dispute will depend on the circumstances of each case and the child's age and maturity. No breach of Article 8 was found. The Court did uphold a breach of Article 14 in that German courts placed a heavier burden on an unmarried father than a divorced father.

In *P, C and S v UK* (2002), the Court considered care and adoption proceedings taken to remove a baby from a mother suspected of harming the child because she suffered from Munchhausen by Proxy Syndrome. Article 8 was held to have been violated due to deficiencies in procedures including the lack of the mother's involvement in the decision-making process given the serious nature of what was at stake. An Article 6 violation was also held to exist due to the lack of access to legal representation, given the complexity and importance of the proceedings.

In *Venema v the Netherlands* (2002), the Court examined a similar question where a child was separated from her parents due to suspicions that a mother suffered Munchhausen by Proxy Syndrome. The Court accepted that in an emergency there may be circumstances where the urgency of situation and the need to protect the child justify failure to involve those with custody of a child in the decision making process. However, the Court went on to say that national authorities must consider whether such circumstances exist before taking action to remove a child without prior contact or consultation. This would entail looking at whether a careful assessment of the actions to be taken, their impact and alternatives had been made. In the circumstances of this case, it would have been possible to have sought the views of the parents before making an order to remove the child and the decision was contrary to the rights protected under Article 8.

In *K and T v Finland* (2000), the Court has acknowledged that, when making emergency care orders, it may not be possible to involve the relevant family members in the decision making process. Nonetheless, in such cases, the care order should be seen as a temporary and interim measure which will be reviewed periodically. This will then allow greater involvement of those affected in any further decisions.

The Court of Appeal in England in re *B and M (Children)* (2002) examined the question of a court's approach to ensuring the implementation of a care plan in conformity with Article 8. In this decision, the Court of Appeal set out a number of principles about the relationship between the Children Act 1989 and Article 8, namely that:

■ a respect for family life is fundamental to the philosophy underpinning both the Convention and Children Act;

■ care order is a serious interference with the right of respect for family life, not only for parents but also, more importantly, for children. The interference is more serious still if only minimal contact is permitted between parents and the child or if contact is refused altogether;

■ the most serious interference is an adoption order which finally and irrevocably brings to an end not only the parent's parental responsibility for the child but also the legal relationship between the child and the whole of his family of birth. On the other hand, not to interfere where interference is called for may also violate a child's rights (though not in an adoption case), (see *Z v United Kingdom*, 2001);

■ these interferences are committed by two separate and independent public authorities: first, the court which makes the orders and secondly the local authority which decides how to implement them or makes arrangements for the child. Such interference can only be justified under Article 8(2) if three conditions are satisfied:

(i) the interference must be in accordance with the law;

(ii) it must pursue one of the legitimate aims provided for in the article so that compulsory measures of care can be justified for the protection of health or morals or the protection of the rights or interests of the child; and

(iii) it must be necessary in a democratic society so that the reasons given for the interference are relevant and sufficient, must correspond to a pressing social need and must be proportionate to the legitimate aim pursued;

■ a public authority may also act incompatibly with Article 8 in a care case where it fails to take adequate steps to secure for a child who has been deprived of a life with his or her family of birth, a life with a new family to make up for what has been lost.

These principles are likely to have similar force when considering care plans under the Children (NI) Order 1995. *In the matter of J and S (Supervision or a Care Order)* (2001) the High Court in Northern Ireland when granting a supervision order to a health and social services trust noted that the court's approach under Article 8 should be to ensure the minimum interference with family life.

In re *G (Care: challenge to a local authorities decision)* (2003), the High Court in England ruled that the procedural protection provided by Article 8 extends to all stages of decision-making, including after proceedings have come to an end. As a result, a local authority is under a duty to inform parents of the intention to make any significant changes to a care plan and to provide parents with an opportunity to make representations about any proposals.

In Re *S(FC), Re S and Others, Re W and Others,* (2002), the House of Lords held that the court's powers under the Children Act do not extend to making interim orders to supervise a local authority's treatment of children in its care. The Human Rights Act did not allow such a power to be read into the Children Act.

Family life – immigration cases

In Northern Ireland, the interference in home life and family life was considered by the Court of Appeal in re *Donnelly* (2003). The applicant had suffered long-standing intimidation from a neighbour. The intimidation was of a sectarian and paramilitary nature. The Housing Executive refused to evict the perpetrator and instead offered to re-house the victim. The Court of Appeal held that Article 8 creates a positive obligation on a public authority to respect an applicant's private and family life and home. This involved a balance between the interests of the applicant and public interest in effectively managing public housing. These interests included the safety of Housing Executive staff. The Court of Appeal ruled that on the basis of the evidence before it, the Housing Executive had not discharged its duty to take reasonable and appropriate steps to secure the Article 8 rights of the family.

In immigration law, Article 8 may be invoked to argue that separation of a family due to deportation or refusal of entry of family members is unlawful. The Commission has held that the test is whether there are insurmountable obstacles to the couple conducting family life in the country to which a married partner is deported (*Sorabjee v UK*) (1994). The Court has held that this principle can apply to an engaged couple and a divorced father who would be separated from his daughter if deported.

In *Boultif v Switzerland* (2001), the Court set out some general principles to be applied to the deportation of non-national family members where the main obstacle to expelling the applicant was the difficulty for a married couple to stay together and, in particular, for a married partner and/or the children to live in the other's country of origin. In assessing whether expulsion is necessary and pro-

portionate, the Court held that it will consider:

- the nature and seriousness of the offence committed by the applicant;

- the length of the applicant's stay in the country from which he or she is going to be expelled;

- the time elapsed since the offence was committed as well as the applicant's conduct in that period;

- the nationalities of the various individuals concerned;

- the applicant's family situation such as the length of the marriage;

- other factors expressing the effectiveness of the couple's family life;

- whether the other partner knew about the offence at the time he or she entered into a family relationship;

- whether there are children of the marriage;

- the seriousness of the difficulties which the other partner is likely to encounter in the country of origin (although the mere fact that a person might face certain difficulties in accompanying her or his partner cannot in itself exclude an expulsion).

In *Tuquabo-Tekle v the Netherlands* (2005), the Court considered whether the Dutch government's refusal to allow a fifteen-year-old living in Eritrea to join her mother, brothers and sisters who had settled in the Netherlands as a refugee was a violation of Article 8. The Court outlined a number of general principles that apply to family re-unification cases. These principles include that the extent of a state's positive obligation to admit relatives of settled immigrants will vary according to the circumstances of the case and the general interest. Relevant factors to be considered will include the age of the child concerned, the situation in the country of origin and the extent to which a child is dependent on his or her parents. Nonetheless, it is well settled that under the Convention and other international obligations a state has the right to control the entry of non-nationals into its country. Article 8 does not impose a general obligation to authorise family reunion on its territory; however, there may be a particular obligation in the light of circumstances in any individual case. In the case under consideration the Court decided that the refusal to grant a residence permit was a violation of Article 8.

In *Huang and Kashmiri v Secretary for the Home Department* (2007) the House of Lords set out how immigration authorities and appellate bodies should apply Article 8 in immigration cases. In particular, the House of Lords noted the need to consider both the positive duty to show respect for family life and also the negative duty not to unduly interfere with the right. Matters including the applicant's age, health and vulnerability, the closeness and previous history of the family, the person's dependence on financial and emotional support from the family, prevailing cultural traditions and conditions in the country of origin may all be relevant. Given normal reliance on immediate extended family, there will come a point where prolonged or unavoidable separation will inhibit a person's ability to live a full and fulfilling life. Decision-making taking account of Article 8 will often involve questions of proportionality.

Family life – other issues

In *R (Bernard) v Enfield Borough Council* (2001), the applicant had six children and a wife who was severely disabled. The family was homeless and was re-housed in unsuitable, unadapted accommodation. Suitable accommodation was only provided after two years. The High Court in England held that the conditions faced by the applicant were contrary to the right to family and private life. As a result damages were awarded. In *Hanna* (2003), the High Court in Northern Ireland considered whether a local health and social services trust's operation of a waiting list due to resource constraints, was contrary to the right to family and private life. In this case, an 84 year old woman was left in hospital several months after being ready for discharge to a nursing home. The High Court held

that there had been no violation of Article 8 in that the health and social services trust did respect the applicant's private and family life, having regard to the balance to be struck between the interests of the applicant and those of other people placed higher up on the list who had been assessed with more urgent and pressing needs. In *Glass v UK* (2004), the Court held that the decision to impose treatment on a severely disabled child against the express wishes of the mother was an interference with the child's right to family life and physical integrity. The Court held that, in the event of a disagreement between parents and doctors, parental refusal to consent to treatment of a child can only be overridden in an emergency. In other situations the onus was on the health authority to obtain a ruling from the High Court. As a result, a breach of Article 8 had occurred and damages were awarded.

In *F (Adult Patient), Re* (2000) the Court of Appeal in England and Wales had to deal with a difficult situation where social services applied to the court to require an adult with severe mental impairment to live in residential care and to restrict contact with family. The applicant's mother opposed the application. The local authority was concerned with the conditions in the parental home and the ability of the parents to look after the applicant. The question before the Court of Appeal was whether it had any inherent jurisdiction to intervene to decide what was in the best interests of an incapable adult where there was disagreement about the welfare of that individual. The Court of Appeal held it did have jurisdiction to intervene. Under the doctrine of necessity, the courts and/or social services must ensure appropriate care and that restraints are provided to meet the best interests of an adult who lacks capacity. The inherent jurisdiction of courts is limited by the European Convention and the need to respect private and family life when taking appropriate measures to protect the safety and welfare of a child or incapable adult. The Convention requirements must therefore be taken into account when exercising such inherent jurisdiction.

In *R on the application of A and B v East Sussex CC and the Disability Rights Commission (No 2)* (2003), the High Court in England and Wales dealt with a situation where two severely disabled adults wanted to be lifted and moved by hand by their carers. The local authority wanted lifting to be done by a hoist in order to minimise risk to its staff. The High Court held that the Article 8 rights of the applicants were engaged alongside the corresponding rights of the carers which were protected under Article 8(2). The balance between these competing rights was to be assessed on a basis of proportionality. Enhanced weight was to be given to the rights of those who through disability are already deprived of a quality of life available to others. In this case, draft protocols were produced by the local authority to set out the circumstances in which manual lifting would be undertaken. The protocols were eventually agreed by all the parties to the case. The High Court went on to say that a blanket ban on manual lifting (except in circumstances where life was at issue or any other means of lifting was physically impossible) was unlikely to be lawful.

Private life

Private life has been held to include physical and moral integrity.

In *Pretty v UK* (2002) the Court set out its wide definition of the scope of private life contained within Article 8 at paragraph 61:

As the Court has had previous occasion to remark, the concept of 'private life' is a broad term not susceptible to exhaustive definition. It covers the physical and psychological integrity of a person. It can sometimes embrace aspects of an individual's physical and social identity. Elements such as, for example, gender identification, name and sexual orientation and sexual life fall within the personal sphere protected by article 8. Article 8 also protects a right to personal development, and the right to establish and develop relationships with other human beings and the outside world. Though no previous case has established as such any right to self-determination as being contained in Article 8 of the Convention, the Court con-

siders that the notion of personal autonomy is an important principle underlying the interpretation of its guarantees.

The Court has held that legislation governing abortion touches on the sphere of private life in that when a woman is pregnant, her private life becomes closely connected with the developing foetus. In *Tysiac v Poland* (2007) the applicant suffered with severe myopia and there was a danger of serious deterioration as a result of continuing her third pregnancy. She sought a termination. Clinicians could not agree on the extent of the danger and she was not granted a certificate authorising an abortion under Polish law. Subsequently, the baby was born and the applicant's eyesight deteriorated further with an increased risk of her going blind. The Court observed that a country's legislation on abortion relates to the traditional balancing of privacy and public interest. In the case of therapeutic abortion, the Court will assess legislation against the positive obligations to secure the physical integrity of mothers-to-be.

On examining the Polish law, the Court noted that abortion was essentially a criminal offence, without clearly defined procedures to determine whether the legal conditions for a therapeutic abortion were in place. This included no established legal procedures for dealing with a dispute between clinicians on the risk to a pregnant woman. The Court also set out that such legal procedures must be applied swiftly, given that time is a critical factor. Examining all the circumstances surrounding the case and the legal framework in Poland, the Court held that the Polish government had failed to comply with its positive obligations to secure the effective respect for the applicant's private life. As a result, Article 8 was breached and non-pecuniary damages were awarded.

In *X and Y v Netherlands* (1985), the Court upheld a complaint by a person with learning difficulties who could not take legal action following a sexual assault as she lacked legal competence under Dutch law. The Court held that there was a violation under Article 8 as the Dutch authorities had failed to secure respect for her private life. In another case, the Commission decided that a father does not have the right to be consulted about a proposed termination of his partner's pregnancy, as, while this is a possible violation, it is justifiable as necessary to protect the rights of others.

In *Peck v UK* (2003), the Court held that closed-circuit television (CCTV) footage taken by a local council of a man's failed suicide attempt that was subsequently made available to the media was a violation of the applicant's right to privacy. The taking of and dissemination of CCTV footage, of itself, may not be a violation of Article 8 as it may pursue a legitimate aim such as prevention of disorder and crime and pursuit of public safety. However, in this case, disclosure was disproportionate to any legitimate aim in that the applicant had committed no criminal offence and his identity could have been ascertained and consent sought for disclosure or his image hidden by the council or media.

The Court has not normally been prepared to include a gay relationship as covered by family life; instead it has held that it is covered within the ambit of private life. In *Dudgeon v UK* (1981) and *Norris v Ireland* (1988), the Court held that treating gay relationships between men as a criminal offence regardless of age and consent was too wide to be justified by the qualifications contained in Article 8(2). Both cases led to the introduction of legislation decriminalising gay male relationships in both parts of Ireland. In *ADT v UK* (2000), the Court held that criminal charges made against men for homosexual acts in private where more than two people were present and the activities were videoed for private use only were an interference with the right to privacy. In re *McR* (2002), the High Court of Northern Ireland declared a provision of the Offences Against the Person Act 1861 dealing with the offence of buggery to be incompatible with Article 8, where the sexual acts between heterosexual adults were consensual. Legislation has now been amended to deal with this issue.

In *Smith and Grady v UK* (1999), the Court held that investigations by military authorities into the sexual orientation of military personnel and subsequent dismissal were contrary to Article 8 and Article 14 (freedom from discrimination). Two decisions of the Court show that Article 8 also protects the right of a transsexual to have his or her changed sex formally recognised by the government, see *Goodwin v UK* (2002) and *I v UK* (2002). As a result of these cases, legislation protecting the rights of transsexuals was introduced (the Gender Recognition Act 2004). In a further case, *Grant v UK* (2006) the Court held that a post-operative male to female transsexual was entitled to receive a state pension from age 60. The UK government's refusal to recognise this was a violation of Article 8.

In *X v Y (Employment: Sex Offender)* (2004), the Court of Appeal in England upheld the dismissal of an employee cautioned for committing an offence in a public lavatory. The employee had not disclosed the caution. The appellant was a highly regarded employee who worked closely with young people. The Court of Appeal held that the right to private life was not engaged in these circumstances.

In *TP (a minor) re an application for Judicial Review* (2005), the High Court in Northern Ireland considered whether the placing of a young person held on remand in an Intensive Support Unit following an incident in Rathgael Juvenile Justice Centre was contrary to Article 8. The High Court noted that the concept of private life covered physical and psychological integrity, a right to personal development and to establish relationships with others. Restrictions on private and family life were necessary during periods of lawful custody. Nonetheless, the right to respect for private and family life remains and must be balanced against reasonable requirements of imprisonment and regulating a prisoner. In addition, the High Court set out that other relevant international obligations including the UN Convention on the Rights of the Child and the Charter of Fundamental Rights of the European Union can be taken into account in interpreting Article 8. In this case, the initial transfer to the Intensive Support Unit with increased restrictions did not interfere with the right to respect for private life. However, the transfer to the unit lasted for several months and while the issue was kept under review no continuing assessment of the Article 8 issues was undertaken. If Article 8 issues had been kept in view then continuing detention in the Intensive Support Unit would not have automatically have resulted. As a result, a violation of the applicant's right to private life had occurred.

The right to a home

Article 8 does not confer an absolute right to a home: see *Burton v UK* (1996). Nonetheless, some protection is provided. In *Velosa Barreto v Portugal* (1995), the Court held that a landlord does not have an unfettered right to recover possession of rented accommodation. However, the reach of Article 8 in dealing with eviction from accommodation has been the subject of a number of recent decisions. In *London Borough of Harrow v Qazi* (2003), the House of Lords examined whether a decision to take possession proceedings engaged Article 8. Mr Qazi lived with his wife and daughter in local authority accommodation under a joint tenancy. His wife and daughter moved out, gave notice to quit and ended the tenancy. Harrow Borough Council refused Mr Qazi's application for a sole tenancy on the grounds that the accommodation was not appropriate for a single person. The council took legal proceedings to recover the property. During the proceedings Mr Qazi commenced another relationship with a woman who had a child. The House of Lords ruled that Article 8 was engaged and that the accommodation remained Mr Qazi's even after the tenancy had been terminated. However, Article 8 does not guarantee a right to a home but, instead, the right to respect a person's home, which is a different concept. Respect for the home is one of the matters that affect a right to privacy. By a majority, the House of Lords held that the council's right to possession was an absolute right and did not violate the essence of the right to respect for the home under Article 8. Contractual and property rights cannot be displaced by a defence under Article 8 of the Convention. In exceptional cases, however, this may be possible where a local authority has acted unfairly or issued an improper notice. In such cases judicial review will be the appropriate remedy.

In contrast, shortly after the Qazi decision the Court considered a similar issue in *Connors v UK* (2004). In *Connors* the applicants were gypsies with a licence to occupy a plot at a caravan site providing they did not cause a nuisance to others using the site. The council served a notice to quit and sought possession of the land on the grounds that the family had caused a nuisance. The family was subsequently evicted. The legal procedures did not require the council to prove any of the allegations of causing a nuisance. Instead, the council only had to give sufficient notice to quit. The Court held there was a violation of Article 8. In particular, there was a positive obligation to facilitate the gypsy way of life. The legal framework governing occupation of local authority pitches did not provide sufficient procedural safeguards. The serious interference with the applicant's rights required very weighty reasons of public interest as justification. The Court was not persuaded that local authority gypsy sites would be unmanageable if a requirement to establish reasons for eviction of long-standing occupants was introduced. In *Connors* the Court took a different line from its earlier decisions.

In *Buckley v UK* (1996), the concept of home was broadly interpreted to include land and a caravan owned and occupied by a travelling family. In this case, however, the refusal of a local authority to grant planning permission to enable the family to live on the land in accordance with tradition was not contrary to Article 8. In *Chapman v UK* (2001), the Court decided that living in caravans was an integral part of gypsy life and ethnic identity and eviction proceedings for breach of planning permission and planning decisions interfered with family and private life. The Court, however, went on to hold that domestic authorities have a wide margin of appreciation when assessing planning conditions on specific sites. In these cases, a legitimate aim was being pursued, namely the protection of the rights of others by maintaining the environment. The strong environmental factors were held to outweigh the applicant's individual interests. The Court also held that Article 8 could not be interpreted to mean that an adequate number of suitably equipped sites for the travelling community must be provided as the article does not give an absolute right to a home. *Connors v UK* (2004) is arguably distinguishable from these cases as the family had been in long-term occupation of the site.

The Court recently declared inadmissible the case of *Codona v UK* (2006) on the grounds that the application was clearly without merit. The applicant, a gypsy, had moved with her extended family on to a site controlled by a local authority. This was in breach of planning regulations. The council obtained a court order to remove the family but agreed to deal with the family's homelessness application. The applicant set out that she had an aversion to bricks and mortar accommodation which would have led to the separation of parts of the extended family. She wanted to live in a caravan with the support of her extended family around her. The council decided it had no land to offer and in the short term could only provide bed and breakfast accommodation. In its inadmissibility decision the Court noted that Article 8 did not encompass a right to be provided with a home, let alone a specific type or category of home. The scope of any positive obligation to house a homeless person is limited. The Court accepted in principle that there could be a positive obligation under Article 8 to facilitate the gypsy way of life and that an aversion to bricks and mortar formed part of that way of life. However, no alternative caravan sites were available. To impose a positive obligation to create a site (or enough sites to meet demands) would go beyond the limited obligations established in earlier case law. The council had complied with any positive obligation it had by attempting to find an official site and was not required to find caravan accommodation where no sites exist. This case illustrates the limit that Article 8 places on positive obligations owed by housing authorities when dealing with gypsy or traveller families.

In *Kay and Others and Another (FC) v London Borough of Lambeth and Others, Price and Others (FC) v Leeds City Council* (2006), the House of Lords has taken the opportunity to resolve the inconsistency between its own decision in *Qazi* and that of the Court in *Connors*. In *Leeds City Council* the House of Lords dealt with the eviction of gypsies unlawfully occupying land owned by the City Coun-cil. The House of Lords held that Article 8 does not provide a defence to possession claims unless there are exceptional circumstances. In *Kay*, the House of Lords decided that *Qazi* was correctly decided and that Article 8 defences concerning personal circumstances should be struck out. An Article 8 defence should only be entertained where a serious arguable legal point is raised that a possession order would be incompatible with Article 8 or that a housing authority's decision to seek possession would be an improper use of their powers. In particular, in a key part of the judgement the House of Lords said:

> *A defence which does not challenge the law under which the possession order is sought as being incompatible with Article 8 but is based only on the occupier's personal circumstances should be struck out . . . [if] the requirements of the law have been established and the right to recover possession is unqualified. The only situations in which it would be open to the court to refrain from proceeding to summary judgment and making the possession order are these: (a) if a seriously arguable point is raised that the law which enables the court to make the possession order is incompatible with Article 8, the county court in the exercise of its jurisdiction under the Human Rights Act 1998 should deal with the argument in one or other of two ways: (i) by giving effect to the law, so far as it is possible for it [to] do so under section 3, [of the Human Rights Act] in a way that is compatible with Article 8, or (ii) by adjourning the proceedings to enable the compatibility issue to be dealt with in the High Court; (b) if the defendant wishes to challenge the decision of a public authority to recover possession as an improper exercise of its powers at common law on the ground that it was a decision that no reasonable person would consider justifiable, he should be permitted to do this provided again that the point is seriously arguable.*

Kay is likely to be appealed to the European Court of Human Rights.

In *Blecic′ v Croatia* (2004), the Court held that the obtaining of a possession order against a tenant who had been absent from her home for six months due to civil disturbance was an interference with her right to respect for her home. However, the Court considered the interference was justified in that it pursued a legitimate aim, namely meeting the housing needs of its citizens.

In *Gunter v South Western Staffordshire Primary Care Trust* (2005), the High Court in England held that the trust was entitled to use a voluntary organisation to provide nursing care services to a patient. However, in deciding to move the applicant into a residential setting to save money, the trust had failed to carry out a lawful Article 8 balancing exercise giving proper weight to the advantages of the applicant remaining at home.

Environmental cases

The right to enjoy a home free from interference has given rise to challenges on environmental grounds, for example excessive noise and pollution in *Lopez Ostra v Spain* (1994), *Guerra v Italy* (1998) and *Powell and Rayner v UK* (1990).

In *Fadeyeva v Russia* (2005), the Court dealt with an applicant who lived 450 metres from a steel-making plant. The government implemented a resettlement scheme after finding the concentration of toxic substances in the air of the town exceeded acceptable norms on many occasions. The applicant was not offered resettlement elsewhere and pursued her claim without success in domestic courts. The applicant complained to the Court that the failure to protect her private life and home from severe environmental pollution was a breach of Article 8. The Court held that for a claim to fall within Article 8 it must directly affect the applicant's home, private or family life and the adverse affects must attain a certain minimum level. To prove this level of interference an applicant may rely on the co-existence of sufficiently strong, clear and concordant inferences or other similar presumptions of fact which are not rebutted. The Court asserted its willingness to be flexible when considering the difficulties of providing evidence given the substantial

issues involved. In this case, although there was no medical evidence directly linking her ill health to the toxins produced by the steel plant, the Court was prepared to accept that prolonged exposure made the applicant more vulnerable to ill-health. As a result, the applicant's claim fell within the scope of Article 8. The Court went on to hold that the interference could not be justified under Article 8(2). It was held that the continued operation of the plant was a legitimate aim and in the economic interests of the state. However, the authorities had not struck a fair balance between the interests of the applicant and the community as a whole. In particular, the authorities had not done enough to reduce industrial pollution to acceptable levels or offer an effective solution to allow the applicant to move. As a result, the Court awarded non-pecuniary damages to the applicant. This case illustrates the positive obligation on a government adequately to regulate the environment where pollution has an adverse impact on the quality of life on individuals and communities.

In *Hatton v UK* (2003), the Court considered whether night flights over Heathrow were in breach of Article 8. The Grand Chamber of the Court noted that Article 8 can apply in environmental cases where pollution is directly caused by the state or is due to the state's responsibility for failing to regulate private industry. In examining environmental issues, a fair balance has to be struck between the competing interests of the individual and of the community as a whole. In this instance, the community interests were the economic wellbeing of the country. The Court held that it was entitled to examine the substantive merits of the government's decision and scrutinise the decision-making process to ensure due weight had been given to the interests of the individual. On the substantive merits, the state is entitled to a wide margin of appreciation in reaching its decision. In this case, the Court held that the government had struck a fair balance on both substantive and procedural issues having consulted widely, undertaken considerable research into the impact of night flights on sleep patterns of those living nearby and modified original proposals to place stricter limitations on night flights.

In *Moreno Gomez v Spain* (2004), the Court held a violation of Article 8 where an applicant had endured excessive noise from bars and discotheques situated in her local area. The local City Council had commissioned a report that confirmed that noise levels exceeded permitted standards and were unacceptable. As a result, the council placed a ban on new activities that would increase noise in the locality. Nonetheless, the council granted a new licence to a discotheque to be opened in the building in which the applicant lived.

Challenges on environmental issues will almost certainly continue to arise under both the Convention and Human Rights Act.

In *re Landlord's Association for Northern Ireland and Others* (2005), the High Court observed that the right to respect for the home is not confined to physical breaches and can extend to noise, smells and other interferences which prevent a person from enjoying the amenities in his or her home.

Right to correspondence

The Court has considered a number of challenges around interception of correspondence, telephone tapping and other surveillance. As a result of cases including *Malone v UK* (1984) and *Halford v UK* (1997), the government had to introduce legislation, the Regulation of Investigatory Powers Act 2000, to provide some safeguards for individuals. The question of surveillance in the workplace without consent and the use of such evidence in disciplinary proceedings is likely to be a significant issue affected by the Human Rights Act.

Access to personal records has also been considered under Article 8. In *Gaskin v UK* (1989), the refusal to provide access to a social services personal file to a person who had been in care all his life was considered. The Court concluded that conflicting interests must be balanced and that independent adjudication was necessary to decide whether disclosure was justifiable. The absence of such independent scrutiny was deemed contrary to the Convention.

In MG *v UK* (2002), the applicant sought access to social services records including whether he had been on the at-risk register or his father had ever been investigated or convicted of crimes against children. The Court held that the failure to provide the information and the absence of any appeal violated Article 8. As a result, damages were awarded for the violation up until 1 March 2000 when, the Court noted, an independent right of appeal had been introduced. In the High Court in England, the procedures for disclosure of adoption records by a voluntary adoption agency were examined in light of Article 8. The case, *Gunn Rosso v Nugent Care Society and Secretary of State for Health* (2001), noted that a balancing act had to be conducted between disclosure and confidentiality. It was held that the Secretary of State had neither the power to force disclosure of records nor a duty to provide for an appeal procedure if disclosure was not forthcoming. The legislation in England and Wales was held to be compatible with Article 8.

In *McConway v Northern Ireland Prison Service and Chief Constable* (2004), the Court of Appeal dismissed a challenge to a decision of the Northern Ireland Prison Service refusing to provide security clearance for the applicant to work in prison on the basis of information it had received from the police. The Court of Appeal upheld the High Court decision that a vetting system in public employment covering security was a legitimate policy aim and the policy on creation and release of security records was proportionate. Article 8 was held not to be engaged and if it did apply then the protections contained in Article 8(2) would have come into effect.

Article 9

FREEDOM OF CONSCIENCE

1. Everyone has the right to freedom of thought, conscience and religion; this right includes freedom to change his religion or belief and

freedom, either alone or in community with others and in public or private, to manifest his religion or belief, in worship, teaching, practice and observance.

2. Freedom to manifest one's religion or beliefs shall be subject only to such limitations as are prescribed by law and are necessary in a democratic society in the interests of public safety, for the protection of public order, health or morals, or for the protection of the rights and freedoms of others.

Article 9 permits no restriction whatsoever in relation to the private practice of a person's thought, conscience or religion. The permissible restrictions under Article 9(2) only apply to the freedom to manifest one's religion. These restrictions (although similar) are less extensive than those available under Articles 8, 10 and 11. Under section 13 of the Human Rights Act, a court and a tribunal must have regard to the importance of a religious organisation's right to freedom of thought, conscience and religion in dealing with any questions under the Act.

Article 9 has been invoked in relatively few complaints; of these most have involved religion, prison restrictions and conscientious objection. On the interference with freedom of religion the Court has traditionally provided considerable scope for states to interfere with the right under the qualifications contained within Article 9(2).

In *Martin Choudhury v UK* (1991), the Commission held there was no obligation on a state to protect its citizens from offence caused by other private individuals. The applicant had complained about the lack of legal redress against the author Salman Rushdie following the publication of the book *Satanic Verses*. The applicant argued that there should be protection from attack for the Moslem religion. The Commission ruled there was no direct interference with the applicant's freedom to manifest his religion or belief and no requirement on a state to have blasphemy laws against all religions. The Commission also held that blasphemy laws that extended to the Christian religion only did not violate Article

14 (freedom from discrimination). The Court might take a different line if such a case arose again in the future.

In *Leyla Sahin v Turkey* (2004), the Court held that a ban applied by the University of Istanbul on students wearing Islamic headscarves or beards was not contrary to Article 9. In particular, the Court held the ban was prescribed by law and pursued the legitimate aim of protecting the rights and freedom of others and protecting public order. As a result, the ban was within the margin of appreciation allowed to a state taking into account that the rules on this issue varied from country to country. The principles of secularism were held to be consistent with the values underpinning the Convention. This case would probably justify the banning of football tops and certain football colours from being worn in some public places in Northern Ireland.

In *Begum v Head Teachers and Governors of Denbigh High School* (2006), the House of Lords considered whether a school-uniform policy which banned the jilbab though permitted the wearing of the shalwar kameeze and headscarves was contrary to Article 9 and the right to education under Article 2 of Protocol 1. The House of Lords noted the fundamental importance of the right to freedom of thought, conscience and religion in a pluralist, multi-cultural society and that Article 9 protects both the right to hold a belief, which is absolute, and a right to manifest a belief, which is qualified. In reviewing the European Court of Human Rights case law, the House of Lords observed that what constitutes interference with Article 9 will depend on the circumstances of the case including the extent to which in such circumstances a person can reasonably expect to be at liberty to manifest his or her beliefs in practice. By a majority the House of Lords held there was no interference with Shabina Begum's Article 9 rights. In any event, the House of Lords held unanimously that any interference was justified. The House of Lords held there was no right to be educated at a particular school and the applicant could have moved to a different school where wearing the jilbab was permitted. As such the uniform policy did not breach Shabina Begum's right to manifest her religion.

In re *Parsons' Application* (2003), the Court of Appeal in Northern Ireland was asked to consider whether the legislation which guaranteed that 50 per cent of new recruits into the Police Service of Northern Ireland was Catholic was contrary to Article 9 and Article 14 (freedom from discrimination). In dismissing the application, the judgment noted again that the right to hold a religious belief is unqualified but the right to manifest it is qualified.

The failure to appoint the applicant was not due to religion, but was a consequence of a failure to reach a required standard for appointment, even though other applicants who were Catholic were appointed without meeting the same standard. No constraint had been placed on the applicant's freedom to hold and espouse a religious belief. In particular, the Court of Appeal held that an act which disadvantaged an applicant due to adherence to a particular religion was not *per se* an invasion of freedom to hold the religion under Article 9(1) of the Convention. Unlawful state interference with religious belief could include discrimination based on having (or not having) a religion, legal proscription of membership of certain religions or beliefs, coercion to get a person to reveal his or her religion or beliefs or the use or threat of physical or penal sanctions to force someone to adhere to or recant beliefs. To engage Article 9(1) the invasion of freedom must be sufficiently substantial when considering the level of disadvantage or coercion applied to a person to reveal his or her religious beliefs. In the circumstances of this case the applicant had a choice which was reasonable to exercise, namely to seek other employment. As a result, the disadvantage was not sufficient to engage Article 9.

Many of the cases considered under Article 9 have involved the rights of Jehovah's Witnesses. In *Kokkinakis v Greece* (1993), the Court held that a law which criminalised activities designed to persuade people to become Jehovah's Witnesses was disproportionate to the need to protect the rights of others. In *Manoussakis and Others v Greece* (1998), a conviction of a Jehovah's Witness for setting up a place of worship without government authorisation was also held to be contrary to Article 9. The freedom to manifest a religion does not restrict the right of a church to expel those who flout the rules of the church (*X v Denmark* 1976) as such individuals can set up their own church or form of religious worship.

In a child custody case, *Hoffman v Austria* (1992), the Court found a violation of the Convention where a mother was denied custody on grounds of being a Jehovah's Witness. The Court held this to be contrary to Articles 8 and 14.

Where there is a conflict between rights protected under the Convention, the Court has held that strong regard must be given to religious beliefs in deciding priority between rights. In *Otto-Preminger Institute v Austria* (1994), the government had interfered with the manager of the Institute's Article 10 freedom by seizing a film due to be shown at the Institute that was considered to offend the religious feelings of Catholics (who were the majority of the people in the region where the applicant sought to show the film). The Court supported the interferences with the applicant's rights as necessary for the protection of the religious rights and freedoms of others. The Court held that the government has a responsibility to ensure the peaceful enjoyment by holders of religious beliefs of their rights under Article 9.

A series of complaints have concerned the lack of respect by government for individual conscientious objection to military service. The Commission, however, rejected all such complaints, relying upon the provisions of Article 4, which specifically envisages the possibility of military service being compulsory. In countries where compulsory military service exists, Article 9 does not require substituted civilian service: see *A v Switzerland* (1984). Where such substituted service exists, a person cannot resist it by invoking Article 9.

A number of complaints concerning the restrictions placed on prisoners in the observance of their religious or conscientious beliefs have been considered. These include respect for the worship and dietary practices of an Orthodox Jew, restrictions on access to religious or philosophical books, the growing of a beard, the wearing of prison clothes, and the religious objection to the cleaning of a prison floor.

In all such cases to date, the Court has been prepared to allow a sufficient margin of appreciation to validate the restriction within Article 9(2). The Court has also considered the question of time off for religious observance of a school teacher to attend Friday prayers at the mosque. In *Ahmad v UK* (1982), the Commission ruled that an employer's refusal to allow time off was reasonable. The Commission appears to have been heavily influenced by the fact that the need for time off had not been raised at either interview or during the first few years of employment. In *Copsey v WHB Devon Clays Ltd* (2005), the Court of Appeal in England and Wales considered a case where a Christian had his employment contract varied to require Sunday working if necessary. The applicant argued that Article 9 had been breached. In dismissing the case the Court of Appeal noted that European case law suggests that Article 9 is not engaged in the context of an employee who raises concerns about hours of work.

Article 10

FREEDOM OF EXPRESSION

1. Everyone has the right to freedom of expression. This right shall include freedom to hold opinions and to receive and impart information and ideas without interference by public authority and regardless of frontiers. This article shall not prevent states from requiring the licensing of broadcasting, television or cinema enterprises.

2. The exercise of these freedoms, since it car-

ries with it duties and responsibilities, may be subject to such formalities, conditions, and restrictions of penalties as are prescribed by law and are necessary in a democratic society, in the interests of national security, territorial integrity or public safety, for the prevention of disorder or crime, for the protection of health or morals, for the protection of the reputation or rights of others, for preventing the disclosure of information received in confidence, or for maintaining the authority and impartiality of the judiciary.

Article 10 must be read in conjunction with section 12 of the Human Rights Act which provides that courts and tribunals must have particular regard to the importance of freedom of expression and that, where an action relates to journalistic, literary or artistic material, then the availability of that material, the public interest in publishing the material and any relevant privacy code must be taken into account. In addition, Article 10 is often strongly linked to Article 11 (freedom of assembly): see *Stankov and United Macedonian Organisation Ilinden v Bulgaria* (2001) discussed in further detail in the review of Article 11.

Scope

The Court has emphasised that freedom of expression is itself a fundamental safeguard for the protection of other human rights; it is generally only through the public condemnation of human rights abuses that they are eradicated. It is also to be protected in its own right. In *Oberschlik v Austria* (1991), the Court noted that:

> *Freedom of the press affords the public one of the best means of discovering and forming an opinion of the ideas and attitudes of political leaders . . . freedom of political debate is at the very core of the concept of a democratic society which prevails throughout the Convention.*

In *Steel and Morris v UK* (2005), the applicants had

been sued by McDonalds for libel after distributing leaflets outside a branch. The Court noted that there was a strong public interest in allowing small campaigning groups to contribute to public debate. Although they must act in good faith and provide accurate and reliable information, a level of hyperbole would be tolerated. It was not, in principle, incompatible with Article 10 to place an onus on a defendant to prove on the balance of probabilities the truth of any public statements made. Large public companies have a right to defend themselves though such companies knowingly and inevitably lay themselves open to close scrutiny and the limits of acceptable criticism are broad. In providing a remedy such as defamation there must be procedural and equality of arms to safeguard free speech and open debate. The award of damages in this case was disproportionate to the legitimate aim served and contrary to Article 10. This case may allow individuals access to legal aid when defending a libel action in certain circumstances.

Article 10 does not, however, provide for untrammelled freedom of expression, with Article 10(2) placing significant fetters on this right. Nonetheless, restrictions on freedom of expression must be strictly proved.

Article 10 has a close relationship with Articles 8, 9 and 11, in that freedom of expression overlaps freedom of thought and conscience, the right to peaceful assembly and the right to non-interference with correspondence. Cases taken under Article 10 can also include claims of violations of other articles.

Freedom of expression includes the right to make speeches or write articles that are offensive or likely to cause offence. In *Handyside v UK* (1976), a publisher was prosecuted for publishing a book intended for children at school which included controversial sexual material. The Court held that:

> *Freedom of expression is applicable not only to 'information' or 'ideas' that are favourably received or regarded as inoffensive or as a matter of indifference, but also to those that offend, shock or disturb the state or any sector of the population. Such are the demands of . . . pluralism, tolerance and broadmindedness, without which there is no democratic society.*

In *Marlow v UK* (2000), the Court held that the prosecution of an author whose book encouraged people to grow cannabis was not contrary to Article 10. In this case, the prosecution was deemed justifiable by the Court on the grounds that it pursued the legitimate aim of preventing crime and was a proportionate response to a pressing social need.

Restrictions on the expression of racist ideas have been upheld as legitimate on the grounds that such prohibitions protect the rights of others. In *Norwood v UK* (2004), the Court declared inadmissible an application challenging the prosecution of a regional organiser of the British National Party who had displayed a large poster at his home that was offensive to Muslims. The Court observed that Article 17 of the Convention provides that the Convention must not be interpreted as giving rights to individuals or groups to destroy the rights and freedoms of others. This provision has a general aim of preventing individuals or groups with totalitarian aims from exploiting for their own ends the principles covered by the Convention. Freedom of expression guaranteed under Article 10 could not be invoked in a way that was contrary to Article 17. The application was held to be manifestly unfounded and declared inadmissible. However, in *Jersild v Denmark* (1994), the Court held that a journalist should not have been prosecuted for aiding and abetting race hatred by broadcasting the views of young self-proclaimed racists in a documentary. In this case, the journalist had produced a serious documentary with alternative views to racism being broadcast and he had not associated himself with the racist comments. The prosecution was disproportionate to the aim of protecting the right of expression. This was so, in spite of the domestic court emphasising the importance of combating race discrimination.

This Article can also cover access to information. In *R (Wagstaff) v Secretary of State for Health* (2001), the High Court in England upheld a claim that the decision to hold a private inquiry into the murders carried out by Dr Harold Shipman was contrary to the right to receive information and the restriction could not be justified.

In *Open Door Counselling Ltd and Dublin Well Woman Centre Ltd v Ireland* (1992), the Court considered the legitimacy of a court injunction preventing the two voluntary organisations from providing information on access to abortion facilities outside Ireland. The Court held that the absolute nature of the injunction and its scope was so wide as to be disproportionate and not justifiable under Article 10(2).

Freedom of expression of particular groups has led to a number of actions before the Court. In *Goodwin v UK* (1996), the Court considered a journalist's right to protect a source after a court order had been obtained compelling disclosure. The Court held that this was a basic condition of press freedom and the order violated Article 10 and was outweighed by the public interest in protecting the source. This is an area where the law is continuing to develop in domestic courts.

Public criticism

In other cases, the Court has held that the boundaries for acceptable criticism of politicians is wider than other individuals in that politicians place themselves in a position of public scrutiny: see *Oberschlik v Austria* (1991). In contrast, restrictions on criticism of the judiciary are more narrowly construed given the need to protect the impartiality of the judiciary.

The Court has held that any restrictions on freedom of expression on legal representatives during legal proceedings should be narrowly construed. In effect, any other type of approach may encroach on an individual client's right to a fair hearing under Article 6. In *Steur v Netherlands* (2003), a lawyer in court proceedings accused a social security investigations officer of applying unacceptable pressure on a client. The investigations officer complained about the lawyer's conduct to the local Bar Association who partly upheld the complaint but imposed no penalty. The Court held that Article 10

had been violated in that the lawyer's criticism had been confined to the courtroom and no attempt had been made by the disciplinary body to ascertain whether it had been made in good faith. Alhough no sanction had been applied to the lawyer, the decision by the disciplinary body could have had an adverse affect on the way the lawyer pursued his professional duties to represent his client's interests in future.

Political activity

The compatibility of political activity with certain occupations has also given rise to case law. In *Vogt v Germany* (1995), the Court had to consider the dismissal of the applicant from her post as a school teacher as a result of her membership of the German Communist Party. It was claimed that this activity was incompatible with the duty of loyalty that the applicant, as a civil servant, owed to the Constitution. The Court noted that civil servants enjoyed the protection of Article 10. It then ruled that the dismissal of the applicant was not proportionate to the legitimate aim pursued and constituted a violation of Article 10 on a number of grounds. First, no other member state of the Council of Europe imposed such a strict duty of loyalty, which applied to all civil servants irrespective of function or rank. Second, the duty did not distinguish between service or private life. Third, the dismissal of the applicant was a very severe measure as it would deprive her of the opportunity to practise her profession. Moreover, the applicant's post did not involve security risks and she had not made any anti-constitutional statements. The Court distinguished a number of other cases concerning the dismissal of teachers from the civil service on the basis that they concerned a right of access to the civil service which had been deliberately omitted from the Convention. Article 11 was also held to be violated.

The case of *Ahmed and Others v UK* (1998) considered certain regulations which prohibited local government employees from engaging in specific types of political activity, including speaking in public and publishing materials in support of a political party. The Court considered that the regulations were a valid response to cases of abuse of power by some local government employees. In finding no violation of Article 10, the Court noted that the regulations did not intend to silence all current or political matters and only applied to carefully defined groups of senior officials (for example, teachers were excluded from the regulations).

In Re *McKinney's application* (2006), the Court of Appeal in Northern Ireland considered whether civil service rules governing employees' right to stand in elections and retain employment were a breach of Article 10. The Court of Appeal dismissed the application and held that although the restrictions applied and had interfered with the applicant's right to freedom of expression under Article 10 they were nonetheless justified. In this case, the applicant was on a low civil service grade and required to resign if he wanted to stand as a candidate for the Northern Ireland Assembly and if unsuccessful apply for reinstatement which would be at the discretion of his employer.

The impact of Article 10 on political parties' freedom of expression and state funding has also been examined. In Re *Sinn Féin's application* (2004), the Court of Appeal ruled that the withholding of statutory-based policy development grants from Sinn Féin for failing to take the Parliamentary oath of allegiance was lawful. The Court of Appeal ruled that Sinn Féin had not demonstrated any restriction on its ability to hold or express opinions or to receive or distribute information, therefore the level of restriction required to constitute a breach of Article 10 did not have to be decided. Sinn Féin made clear that it would not take seats in the Westminster Parliament even if the oath of allegiance was modified, therefore failure to pay grants to assist in policy formulation during daily Parliamentary activity could not amount to a breach of Article 10.

In *R v Shayler* (2002), the House of Lords held that relevant parts of the Official Secrets Act which allow criminal charges to be brought for disclosure of information by members of the security services were compatible with Article 10. The justification for the restriction was accepted on the basis of the damage caused by disclosures made to unauthorised persons. The defendant was later sentenced to six months' imprisonment.

Artistic and commercial expression

Artistic freedom has also been protected under Article 10. In *Muller v Switzerland* (1988), an artist had three paintings confiscated from an exhibition which depicted sexual acts between men and animals. The artist was prosecuted along with the organisers of the exhibition. The Court held that Article 10 covered artistic expression and such expression was essential in a democratic society and undue restrictions should not be allowed. Nonetheless, the Court did not find a violation of Article 10 and did not interfere with the Swiss government's decision that the prosecution was necessary for the protection of public morality.

Commercial expression may also be protected. In *Belfast City Council v Miss Behaving Ltd* (2007), the House of Lords considered the question of the City Council's refusal to grant a licence to trade as a sex shop. The Court of Appeal in Northern Ireland had held that the Council's failure to conduct a balancing exercise between M Ltd's Article 10 rights and matters that might justify interference under Article 10 (2) led to the Council's decision being unlawful. The House of Lords overturned the Court of Appeal's decision, finding that although Article 10 was engaged (albeit at a low level), the decision was well within the qualified right within Article 10 (2). The House of Lords noted that the margin of appreciation granted to public authorities in these matters was broad in scope. Moreover, the House of Lords considered that the procedural failure to examine Article 10 rights did not render the decision unlawful as found by the Court of Appeal. Instead, it is the substantive outcome rather than the procedural issue which must be examined in the light of Article 10 rights.

Article 11

FREEDOM OF ASSOCIATION, PEACEFUL ASSEMBLY AND THE RIGHT TO JOIN A TRADE UNION

1. Everyone has the right to freedom of peaceful assembly and to freedom of association with others, including the right to form and to join trade unions for the protection of his interests.

2. No restrictions shall be placed on the exercise of these rights other than such as are prescribed by law and are necessary in a democratic society in the interests of national security or public safety, for the prevention of disorder or crime, for the protection of health or morals or for the protection of the rights and freedoms of others. This article shall not prevent the imposition of lawful restrictions on the exercise of these rights by members of the armed forces, of the police or of the administration of the state.

Article 11 provides an important right to demonstrate and take other forms of collective action. It does not provide an absolute right to assemble, rather a right to peaceful assembly. This right can be restricted in a number of circumstances. This Article may be invoked in terms of the right of the Orange Order and other loyal institutions to march along traditional routes. However, given the fetters contained in Article 11(2), there is no certainty as to the outcome of any legal action. To date, no successful legal action has been taken by the Orange Order or other loyal institutions to argue a breach of Article 11 against a decision of the Parades Commission.

Underlying principles

In *Stankov and United Macedonian Organization Ilinden v Bulgaria* (2001), the Court set out a number of important principles that govern the interpretation of Article 11. The Court noted that, although Article 11 only protects the right to peaceful assembly and does not cover a demonstration where the organisers and participants have violent intentions, freedom of assembly and freedom of expression are necessarily linked. Both concepts are essential foundations of a democratic society and a basic condition for societal and individual development. Article 11 is designed to protect demonstrations that may annoy or give offence to people opposed to the organisers' aims. The restrictions contained in Article 11(2) are exhaustive and should be interpreted in a narrow and restricted way. Restrictions imposed on freedom of assembly which are 'necessary in a democratic society' imply an interference which corresponds to a pressing social need and is proportionate to the legitimate aim pursued. A contracting state has a certain margin of appreciation subject to supervision of the Court which can give a final ruling on whether a restriction can be reconciled within Article 11.

The role of the Court will not be to substitute its own views for that of the relevant national government or court but to review the decision in light of Article 11. This does not mean confining itself to examining whether discretion was exercised reasonably carefully and in good faith. Instead, the Court will look at the interference that is being challenged in the light of the case as a whole and decide whether a legitimate aim has been established for a restriction and, if so, whether the restriction is proportionate and the reasons to justify the action are relevant and sufficient. In doing this exercise, the Court will want to be satisfied that the national authorities applied standards in conformity with the principles enshrined in Article 11 and have based any decisions on an acceptable assessment of the relevant facts.

The specific issue in *Stankov* concerned restrictions placed on the activities of a local Macedonian nationalist organisation by the Bulgarian government. In particular, the Bulgarian authorities either refused permission or attached substantial conditions to the holding of meetings. In holding that Article 11 had been violated, the Court said that an organisation asserting a minority nationalist consciousness does not of itself justify an interference with freedom of assembly. The fact that a body is demanding fundamental constitutional and territorial change does not automatically justify a prohibition of the right of freedom of assembly. Sweeping measures to curb freedom of assembly and freedom of expression other than for reasons of incitement to violence or rejection of democratic principles do a disservice to democracy, no matter how shocking, unacceptable and illegitimate the demands seem to the authorities.

Freedom of assembly

Article 11 places a positive obligation on the state to ensure that conditions exist for demonstrations or public meetings to take place peacefully. This requires that reasonable steps be taken to allow demonstrators to attend without fear of being subjected to physical violence by their opponents. In *Plattform 'Ärzte für das Leben' v Austria* (1988), a march was disrupted by counter-demonstrators despite the prior deployment of police by the authorities. The marchers, although subjected to abuse and pelted with eggs and clumps of grass, did not suffer any physical violence. The organisers complained that they had received insufficient police protection for this and a further rally which was similarly disrupted. The Court held that, whilst there was a positive obligation on states to take reasonable and appropriate measures to enable lawful demonstrations to proceed, it did not mean that they were obliged to guarantee this absolutely. The Court found no violation, given the leeway available to states in deciding what was appropriate protection.

In *Appleby and others v UK* (2003), the applicants were campaigning against a decision to build on the only public playing field near a town centre. The group sought to set up a stall to collect signatures in a privately owned shopping mall and were refused permission by the owners who had the powers to exclude anyone from carrying out unauthorised activities on its land. The applicants argued that the government had failed in its positive obligation to protect freedom of speech and assembly. In rejecting this argument, the Court found that the

applicants had alternative ways of getting publicity for their cause and the refusal of permission to gather in a shopping mall did not undermine their Article 10 and Article 11 rights.

Article 11 is not violated by a requirement that public demonstrations obtain a prior licence or other permit. The Court views such a requirement as the corollary of the duty on the authorities to ensure that the assembly is not disrupted so that they have adequate notice to deploy police and to ensure rival demonstrations are scheduled so as not to clash. Any licensing system must not overstep this aim by restricting assemblies for other purposes.

Where the circumstances make it impracticable for a demonstration to proceed peacefully, the state may be entitled to impose a blanket ban upon public assemblies: see *Christians against Racism and Fascism v UK* (1980). In such a situation, the Commission was prepared to scrutinise the reasonableness of the measures. Relevant factors will be the duration of the ban, the extent of its geographical area of application and the categories of groups to which it applies.

Freedom of association

With regard to freedom of association, the Court has held that this extends to organisations of mutual interest. This does not, however, cover the freedom not to belong to professional bodies that regulate medical practitioners, lawyers and engineers. Such organisations are regulatory bodies exercised for the public benefit and not a form of association covered by Article 11.

The right to join a political party has been subject to scrutiny under Article 11. In *United Communist Party v Turkey* (1998), the Court stressed that political parties are a form of association essential for the proper functioning of democracy and that there could be no doubt that they came within the scope of Article 11 even where their activities are inimical to the government. The Court noted that:

> *having regard to the essential role of political parties in the proper functioning of democracy, the exceptions set out in Article 11*

are, where political parties are concerned, to be construed strictly; only convincing and compelling reasons can justify restrictions on such parties' freedom of association. In determining whether a necessity within Article 11(2) exists, the Contracting States possess only a limited margin of appreciation, which goes hand in hand with rigorous European supervision embracing both the law and the decisions applying it, including those given by independent courts.

The applicant party was dissolved by the Turkish Constitutional Court on the basis of its use of the word communist in its name and that it sought to promote separatism by referring to a Kurdish nation and citizen. The Court held that a political party's choice of name cannot in principle justify dissolution in the absence of other relevant and sufficient circumstances. Moreover, it noted that the political party was not advocating separatism but was rather seeking a peaceful and democratic solution to the Kurdish problem by political means. It considered that one of the principal characteristics of democracy is the possibility it offers of resolving a country's problems through dialogue, without recourse to violence.

Democracy thrives on freedom of expression. From that point of view, there can be no justification for hindering a political group solely because it seeks to debate in public the situation of part of the state's population and to take part in the nation's political life in order to find, according to democratic rules, solutions capable of satisfying everyone concerned.

The Court therefore concluded that permanent dissolution of the applicant party, ordered before its activities had even started, and coupled with a ban barring its leaders from discharging any other political responsibility, constituted a violation of Article 11.

In *Refah Parlisi v Turkey* (2003), the Court considered another ban on a political party by the Turkish Constitutional Court. In this case, the ban was held not to be contrary to Article 11. The Court held that political parties must meet two conditions to enjoy

the protection of Article 11. First, when campaigning for changes to state legislation and structures, the means used must be lawful and democratic. Second, the changes sought must be compatible with fundamental democratic principles. It therefore followed that a political party whose leaders incited others to use violence or supported political aims that were inconsistent with the rules of democracy could not rely on the protection of the Convention against sanctions imposed on the organisation.

Trade union rights

Article 11 will be violated if an applicant is denied the right to belong to a trade union. A more contentious question is whether Article 11 encompasses the right not to belong to a trade union. In *Young, James and Webster v UK* (1981), three employees were required to join one of three named trade unions recognised by British Rail. The three men declined to join any of them and were dismissed, refusal to join a trade union where a closed shop operated then being a valid ground for dismissal. They complained that their rights under Article 11 amongst others had been violated. Whilst the Court was of the view that Article 11 did convey a right not to be compelled to join an association or union, it did not rule on this point. It did, however, find that the agreement precluded the applicants from forming or joining another union and post-dated their employment with the company, and that the threat of dismissal was such a serious form of compulsion that, taken together, Article 11 had been violated. The Court considered and rejected the possibility of the facts being justified within Article 11(2). In any event, the domestic statutory law was subsequently changed to ban the closed shop.

Article 11 also safeguards the right of trade unions to look after their members' interests. Governments must not create a legislative environment that is so hostile as effectively to prevent a union's ability to protect its members' interests. However, court decisions have narrowly construed this freedom. In *National Union of Belgian Police v Belgium* (1975), the Court upheld the right of a union to be heard, but not to be automatically included in any consultation process. Likewise, in *Swedish Engine Drivers Union v Sweden* (1976), a union did not have an exclusive right to negotiate collective wage agreements. In *Schmidt and Dahlstrom v Sweden* (1976), the Court emphasised the importance of the right to strike, but said that it may be subject to reasonable restrictions.

In *Wilson and NUJ and Others v UK* (2002), the applicant challenged the practice of employers de-recognising trade unions and ending collective bargaining agreements. As part of this process, employees were asked to sign personal contracts and lose trade union rights or accept a lower pay rise. The Court held this was contrary to Article 11 as legislation which permitted employers to use this approach to undermine trade union membership amounted to a failure of the government to adhere to its positive obligations under Article 11. Nonetheless, the Court found that the lack of a legal obligation obliging employers to enter into collective bargaining or recognise trade unions did not in itself violate Article 11.

Moreover, in *Schettini v Italy* (2000), the Court noted that, although trade unions have a right to be heard and to protect their members' interests, governments are free to choose the means to ensure these goals are met.

Article 11(2) lists permitted restrictions upon the substantive rights in similar terms to those applying to the three preceding Articles. It additionally permits restrictions to be placed on the freedom of assembly, association and membership of trade unions for members of the armed forces, the police and of the administration of the state. The extent of this additional restriction was explored in the complaint lodged by the Civil Service Unions following the UK government's decision in 1984 to prohibit trade union membership amongst its civilian workers at the GCHQ telecommunications interception station. The Court held the complaint inadmissible despite there being little objective evidence that union membership at the establishment compromised national security or was otherwise harmful to the public good. The Court considered that the only requirement for such restrictions to be valid was that they be lawful and the state was not obliged

to establish that the restrictions were necessary in a democratic society. However, the decision should be read alongside the judgment in *Vogt v Germany* (1995). The Court there ruled that the notion of 'administration of the state' should be narrowly interpreted in the light of the post held by the official concerned but did not decide whether teachers were included in this category.

Article 12

THE RIGHT TO MARRY

Men and women of marriageable age have the right to marry and to found a family according to the national laws governing the exercise of this right.

Article 12 is arguably an aspect of the right to family life under Article 8. However, Article 8(2) provides a number of restrictions on the exercise of this right, whereas the right to marry is subject only to the person being of marriageable age and to national laws which cover the exercise of marriage. The role of national law cannot, however, place limitations which have the effect of impairing the very essence of the right to marry. In *Cossey v UK* (1990), a post-operative male to female transsexual complained that, under UK law, she was unable to enter into a marriage with a man. The Court observed that the applicant's inability to marry a woman did not result from any legal impediment. In respect of her inability to marry a man, UK law was held to be in conformity with Article 12 which the Court held was to protect the traditional marriage between persons of opposite biological sex. In *Goodwin v UK* and *I v UK* (2002), the Court held that the failure to allow marriage in these circumstances was a violation of Article 12. In *Bellinger v Bellinger* (2003), the House of Lords ruled that a marriage between a man and a woman who was born as a man was invalid. The Court went on, however, to issue a declaration of incompatibility in respect of section 11(c) of the Matrimonial Causes Act, which prompted Parliament to pass the Gender Recognition Act 2004.

In *B and L v UK* (2005), the Court held that the law which prevented a man from marrying his former daughter-in-law while his son and his son's mother were still alive was in breach of Article 12 of the Convention. This has now been remedied through the Law Reform (Miscellaneous Provisions) (NI) Order 2006.

The right to marry does not carry with it a right to divorce. In *Johnston v Ireland* (1987), the applicant formed a stable relationship for over eight years with another person, but could not get married due to the lack of divorce laws in Ireland at the time. This was held not to be a violation of Article 12.

A number of cases have concerned the rights of prisoners to get married. In *Hamer v UK* (1979), the government's refusal to allow prisoners to marry was held to be a violation of Article 12 where the term of imprisonment would lead to a considerable delay in the right to marry. In *X and Y v Switzerland* (1978), the refusal of authorities to allow conjugal visits between prisoners and their spouses was held to be justified for the prevention of disorder or crime; such cases raise issues under Article 8 as well as Article 12 and if the interference is justified under Article 8(2), then no violation can be found under Article 12. The Court also held in *Dickson v UK* (2006) that the refusal of access to artificial insemination facilities for a prisoner who married while in prison and wished to start a family was not contrary to Article 8 or Article 12.

The principles applied to the question of deportation and its effect on Article 12 rights are similar to those applied to Article 8. An applicant is required to advance credible evidence that, if expelled, his or her partner would not follow or that marriage would be impossible in another country.

Article 13

THE RIGHT TO AN EFFECTIVE REMEDY

Everyone whose rights and freedoms as set forth in this Convention are violated shall have an effective remedy before a national authority notwithstanding that the violation is committed by persons acting in a personal capacity.

Article 13 applies not only to the rights set out in Articles 2 to 12 and Article 14 of the Convention, but also those Protocols ratified by the UK, ie Protocols 1, 4, 6 and 7. Under Article 34, a complaint can only be lodged by a victim of an alleged violation of the Convention and the Protocols. Moreover, a government must not hinder in any way the effective exercise of the right to a complaint: for example, see *Finucane v UK* (2003). In addition, an applicant can only allege a violation of Article 13 when combined with any of the above substantive rights. The Court is not, however, prevented from finding a violation of Article 13 alone. Where a person considers that he or she has been a victim of a violation of one of the substantive rights and the alleged violation is objectively arguable, then Article 13 requires an effective remedy for determining the claim as well as providing the possibility of redress.

Article 13 overlaps with Article 6. In practice, the Court has taken the view that the requirements of Article 13 are less strict than those contained in Article 6 and if a violation of Article 6 is found, then it is not necessary to investigate Article 13. Similarly, the Court considers that if Article 5(4) is violated, then there is no necessity to consider Article 13.

A number of principles have emerged from the case law of the Court as to what constitutes an effective remedy. The authority referred to in Article 13 does not have to be a judicial authority: see *Klass v Germany* (1978) and *Leander v Sweden* (1987). Where an authority is not a judicial body, its powers and the guarantees which it offers are relevant in deciding whether the remedies offered are effective. In *Chahal v UK* (1996), the Court held that proceedings before an advisory panel which covered an appeal against deportation on the basis of national security did not offer sufficient procedural safeguards for the purposes of Article 13. In this case, the review body could only make recommendations to the Home Office, rather than provide absolute guarantees. A single remedy may, by itself, not satisfy the requirements of Article 13. However, when taken together with other remedies provided under national law, they may then be acceptable, see *Leander v Sweden* (1987) and *Silver v UK* (1983).

In deportation cases, Article 13 requires a government to provide an effective form of independent scrutiny of any claim that there exist substantial grounds that deportation to another country will lead to a real risk of inhuman treatment or torture contrary to Article 3. In *Bensaid v UK* (2001), the Court held that judicial review proceedings did provide a remedy compatible with Article 13. In *Smith and Grady v UK* (1999), the Court held that the threshold applied by the High Court and Court of Appeal in England on whether the Ministry of Defence's policy of dismissing gay servicemen and women was set so high that the applicants had no effective remedy under Article 13. Where a person claims that he or she has suffered torture, an effective remedy will involve an investigation capable of leading to identification and punishment of those responsible and effective access for the applicant to the investigatory procedure and, where appropriate, the right to payment of compensation, see *Aydin v Turkey* (1997). In *Z v UK* (2001), the Court held that the failure to provide an effective investigation into a local authority's inhuman treatment of children in care was a breach of Article 13.

In *Keenan v UK* (2001), the Court held that the inability of a prisoner to challenge an award of 28 days of extra imprisonment under prison rules was a breach of Article 13. In addition, the absence of a remedy for the parents to challenge the subsequent suicide in the same case was another violation of Article 13.

There are implied limitations on the scope of Article 13 in the field of state security, including police surveillance. Where, for example, a person's privacy is infringed by surveillance, a strict interpretation of Article 13 would require that he or she has a right to challenge the surveillance and for a domestic court to give a ruling on this point. However, for this to occur, the person would have to know of the alleged violation which could make the surveillance ineffective. The Court has, therefore, required that,

in such cases, the domestic remedy be as effective as it can be, given the particular nature of the problem. In the case of telephone tapping, this has been held to include the person being notified as soon as possible without jeopardising the surveillance. In the case of keeping secret files, the Court has held that this includes supervision by an independent Ombudsperson. In addition, Article 13 does not give the Court the power to quash a criminal conviction.

It is important to note that Article 13 has not been transposed into the Human Rights Act 1998. However, section 8 of the Human Rights Act does allow a court or tribunal to grant remedies within its powers as it considers just. This includes awarding damages, but only where the court or tribunal already has such powers. As a result, criminal courts will not have such powers. Damages awarded must follow the principles used by the Court in Strasbourg to quantify compensation. For tribunals, if existing powers to grant relief are inadequate, then section 7(11) allows a government minister to make rules to extend remedies, but this power has not yet been exercised.

Article 14

FREEDOM FROM DISCRIMINATION

The enjoyment of the rights and freedoms set forth in this Convention shall be secured without discrimination on any ground such as sex, race, colour, language, religion, political or other opinion, national or social origin, association with a national minority, property, birth or other status.

Article 14 is not a free-standing right, in that it must be invoked in tandem with one of the substantive rights set out in Articles 2 to 12 of the Convention and the Protocols. Nevertheless, it is well established that Article 14 can be relied on without having to show one of the other rights has been violated. Instead, it is sufficient to show that the facts fall within the ambit of one or more rights and freedoms contained in the Convention: see *re McDonnell* (2001) *and* re *Parsons* (2002) in the High Court of Northern Ireland as just two examples. The limitation created by freedom from discrimination not being a free-standing right has been long debated within the Council of Europe. An additional protocol (Protocol No 12) was created in November 2000 to introduce freedom from discrimination as a free- standing right. However, the UK government has neither signed nor ratified Protocol 12, arguing that while agreeing in principle that freedom from discrimination should be a free-standing right the protocol is too widely drawn.

Indirect discrimination

Article 14 does require that there must be no discrimination in the delivery of substantive rights within the Convention. The Court has traditionally only dealt with questions of direct discrimination. However in *Hugh Jordan v UK* (2001) at paragraph 154, the Court did suggest that Article 14 extends to questions of indirect discrimination. In *Thlimmenos v Greece* (2000), the Court said at paragraph 44 that:

> *The Court has so far considered that the right under Article 14 not to be discriminated against in the enjoyment of the rights guaranteed under the Convention is violated when states treat differently persons in analogous situations without providing an objective and reasonable justification. However, the Court considers that this is not the only facet of the prohibition of discrimination in Article 14. The right not to be discriminated against in the enjoyment of the rights guaranteed under the Convention is also violated when states without an objective and reasonable justification fail to treat differently persons whose situations are significantly different.*

Although the Court has not made a substantive ruling on whether indirect discrimination is covered by Article 14, it is clear that the time is ripe for clarification of this issue.

Key principles

The list of possible forms of discrimination given in Article 14 is illustrative and not exhaustive. In *Belgian Linguistic (case No. 1)* (1967), the Court laid down basic principles for approaching the issue of discrimination within the Convention, saying:

> *The principle of equality of treatment is violated if the distinction has no objective and reasonable justification. The existence of a justification must be assessed in relation to the aims and effects of the measure under consideration, regard being had to the principles which normally prevail in democratic societies. A difference of treatment in the exercise of a right laid down in the Convention must not only pursue a legitimate aim. Article 14 is likewise violated when it is clearly established that there is no relationship of proportionality between the means employed and the aim sought to be realised.*

The Court will find a violation of Article 14 if the discrimination does not pursue a legitimate aim or cannot be objectively justified. In *Darby v Sweden* (1990), the applicant worked in Sweden for many years without formally registering residence. He was required to pay a church tax for a church to which he did not belong, whereas people in a similar situation who had registered their residence were exempt from the tax. The Court found no legitimate aim for this unequal treatment and, as a result, found Article 14 violated in tandem with Article 1 of Protocol 1.

The Court has taken a very strong stance with regard to discrimination on the basis of sex, as the advancement of equality of the sexes is a major goal of the Council of Europe. In *Van Raalte v Netherlands* (1997), the Court noted that weighty reasons must be put forward before a difference of treatment on the sole ground of sex could be regarded as compatible under the Convention. In this case, the Court held that the levying of contributions from the applicant (a childless man aged over 45) under a child benefit law was discrimination on the basis of sex since childless women of the same age were exempt from the same contributions.

The Court has also been strongly critical in cases of alleged discrimination on the basis of birth and nationality. With regard to nationality, in *Gaygusuz v Austria* (1996), the Court held that the refusal of the authorities to grant to a Turkish applicant the social benefit derived from employee contributions on the grounds of nationality was not based on any objective or reasonable justification. In *R (Morris) v Westminster City Council and First Secretary of State* (2004), the High Court in England declared that a section of the Housing Act 1996 was incompatible with Article 14 of the Convention. The case concerned a British woman with a three-year-old child who was a Mauritian citizen subject to immigration control. Under the Housing Act the child was not eligible for consideration and as a result the mother was not judged to be in priority need as she was deemed to be a single person. The High Court ruled that Article 8 (the right to respect for family life) was engaged, as an aim of homelessness legislation was to prevent families splitting up. The judgment found the relevant section discriminatory on grounds of nationality and without objective justification.

The approach of the Court was matched by the House of Lords in *Ghaidon v Goden-Mendoza* (2004) which held that the failure of a gay man to be awarded a secure tenancy on succession following the death of his partner was contrary to Article 14 read with Article 8. The issue turned on the interpretation of the word spouse in the Rent Act. The Court of Appeal in this case had set out that discrimination was a matter of great constitutional importance and there would be limited judicial deference to Parliament on such issues. The decision also went on to note that greater latitude would be given to the legislature on other social and economic issues. The House of Lords in upholding the Court of Appeal's decision held there was no fair or rational ground for making a distinction between a gay and heterosexual couple. There was no legitimate aim to justify a difference in treatment. Any such treatment would be unacceptable in a modern democratic society at the beginning of the twenty-first century.

A similar view was adopted by the Court in *Karner v Austria* (2003) on the question of whether a succession to a private rented tenancy extended to gay couples. The Court emphasised that differences in treatment based on sexual orientation require particularly serious reasons for justification. The Austrian government argued that the statutory provision was designed to protect the traditional family unit. The Court noted that this was in principle a legitimate and weighty reason. Nonetheless, it was held to be a rather abstract aim and a wide range of concrete measures could be used to implement it. Where the margin of appreciation is narrow, the principle of proportionality between the means employed and the aim being realised is not confined to simply showing the measure chosen was suitable to meet that aim; it must also be demonstrated that it was necessary to exclude gay couples from the scope of the legislation to achieve the aim. The Austrian government had not advanced any such specific arguments to support this conclusion and so the grounds for justification for the discrimination was rejected.

Although the state may lawfully discriminate in the context of immigration control (subject to complying with international law) it cannot unjustifiably treat non-UK nationals differently where the treatment does not concern immigration control. In essence, this was one of the findings of the House of Lords in *A and Others and X and Another v Secretary of State for Home Department* (2004). In this case the House of Lords examined the provision of indefinite detention against non-UK nationals against whom no criminal charges had been brought and where no criminal trial was in prospect. The government had derogated from Article 5 in implementing the arrangements under section 23 of the Anti-terrorism, Crime and Security Act 2001. While the majority held that although there was a public emergency threatening the life of the nation to justify the derogation, the response was not proportionate. In addition, the provision failed to address the question of UK nationals suspected of international links with terrorism and therefore breached Article 14.

Different treatment under Northern Ireland law from that applied to an individual in England, Wales and

Scotland has been held not to be a violation of Article 14. The Court in *Magee v UK* (2001) rejected an argument that the difference in rules governing access of terrorist suspects to lawyers between Northern Ireland and the rest of the United Kingdom was discrimination on grounds of national origin or association with a national minority. The difference in treatment depended on the geographical location where the individual was arrested and the Court found this did not amount to discriminatory treatment within the meaning of Article 14.

In some cases, the unequal treatment of different persons is, in fact, treatment designed to redress an existing inequality. Where groups which occupy a privileged position may be required to compensate for this by accepting additional burdens or restrictions on their rights, this may be found to be permissible. An example of this is *Stec and Others v UK* (2006) where the Grand Chamber of the Court held that tying the reduction or cut-off point to entitlement to industrial injuries benefits Reduced Earnings Allowance and Retirement Allowance to pensionable age was lawful. The restrictions placed on entitlement pursued a legitimate aim and were reasonably and objectively justified. In giving judgement the Court emphasised the general principle that Article 14 does not stop states from treating groups differently in order to correct inequalities. It noted further that a failure to correct inequality through different treatment may in itself be contrary to Article 14. In an earlier admissibility decision the Court held that the right to these industrial Injuries benefits were covered by Article 1 of Protocol 1 which was an important decision in its own right.

Margin of appreciation

The Court will allow governments a certain leeway or margin of appreciation in deciding whether a violation has taken place. This leeway depends on the nature of the matter in question. For example, on issues of taxation, the margin of appreciation is usually quite wide, while issues involving family life or racial bias are much more narrowly construed. The Court will, on occasions, take into account what is happening across the states recognising the

Convention. For example, in *Petrovic v Austria* (1998), the question of the refusal of the Austrian government to grant Parental Leave Allowance to fathers when such a benefit was available to mothers was considered. The applicant alleged a violation of Article 14 taken together with Article 8 (the right to family life). The Court noted that the refusal constituted a difference in treatment on the grounds of sex and that mothers and fathers were in analogous positions as far as taking care of children is concerned. It ruled, however, that the Austrian government had not exceeded the margin of appreciation because of the lack of common ground in this field among the legal systems of contracting states. As a result, there was no violation of Article 14. Given the decision was considering the position as it stood at commencement of proceedings in 1989, it is arguable that a similar challenge now may achieve a different outcome.

In *Barrow v UK* (2006), *Pearson v UK* (2006) and *Walker v UK* (2006), the Court gave three separate judgments which upheld the policy of the government to defer the full introduction of equal pension ages for men and women until 2020 and to stop invalidity benefit being paid to women when reaching pensionable age at 60 while continuing to pay the benefit to men until they reached 65 years of age. The Court held that the policy fell within the government's margin of appreciation and was not in breach of Article 14 and Article 1 of Protocol 1 protecting property rights. In light of the original justification for the difference in treatment (the slowly evolving nature of the change in women's working lives and the absence of a common standard among European States), the Court found that the slow pace of reform and failure to implement change from an earlier date was understandable, particularly given the far-reaching implications of the change for women and the economy in general.

In *Burden and another v UK* (2007) the Court held that the difference in treatment for inheritance tax purposes between siblings who jointly owned property and couples who were married or in a civil partnership was not a violation of Article 14 taken together with Article 1 of Protocol No. 1. In particular, the Court held that the difference in treatment was objectively justified. The Court accepted the UK government's argument that it was pursuing a legitimate aim, namely to promote stable committed heterosexual and gay relationships by providing a survivor a degree of financial security after the death of a spouse or legally recognised partner.

In *McDonnell and Lilly* (2004), the Court of Appeal in Northern Ireland held that a scheme to permit tenants to buy Housing Executive properties which excluded pensioner-type accommodation did not breach Article 14. Although Article 8 was engaged, the Housing Executive had been able to demonstrate that its policy was objectively justified in terms of management of its accommodation. An example of a different approach taken to housing policy can be found in Re *Landlords' Association for Northern Ireland and Others* (2005), where the High Court in Northern Ireland held that a scheme for registering houses in multiple occupation which charged fees for private owners while exempting government-funded organisations was contrary to Article 14.

Social security cases

A number of social security challenges have been launched on the basis of Article 14 allied to other rights. In *Willis v UK* (2002), the Court held that failure to pay a widower an equivalent benefit to Widow's Payment and Widowed Mother's Allowance was contrary to Article 14 read with Article 1 of Protocol 1 of the Convention. The grounds for the discrimination could not be objectively justified and the Court held that there must be particularly weighty considerations to justify any difference in treatment between widows and widowers. In *R (Hooper and others) v Secretary of State for Work and Pensions* (2005), the House of Lords held that the failure to pay a Widow's Pension to a widower could be objectively justified and was therefore not contrary to Article 14 read with Article 8 (the right to family life). On the question of failure to pay a Widow's Payment and Widowed Mother's Allowance, the House of Lords did not disturb an earlier ruling that the provisions governing payment of these benefits were a breach of Article 8 read with Article 14. In addition, in *Runkee* and *White* (2007), the

Court noted that correcting historical inequalities in the labour market by giving special treatment to widows was permissible. As the inequality gradually declined, it was a matter for the legislature to determine when to deal with the matter. The Court would only interfere if the approach was manifestly unreasonable. As a result, there was no breach of Article 14.

In *Hobbs and Others v UK* (2006), the Court held that the difference in treatment between men and women in access to widow's bereavement tax allowance up until 6 April 2000 could not be objectively justified and was a violation of Article 14 read with Article 1 of Protocol 1.

In *Carson and Reynolds v Secretary of State for Work and Pensions* (2005), a challenge was made to the different rates of Income Support and Income-based Jobseeker's Allowance payable to people aged 25 or over and those aged under 25. In *R (Carson) v Secretary of State for Work and Pensions* (2005), the issues concerned the government's policy of not uprating Retirement Pension annually when payable to people living abroad in countries which do not have reciprocal agreements for uprating pensions. The actions were based on Article 14 being read with Article 1 of Protocol 1. Both policies were held to be unlawful. The House of Lords in giving a single judgement on both cases outlined that certain forms of discrimination, for example, race, gender and membership of a political party would rarely provide acceptable grounds for different treatment. However, Article 14 was more widely drawn. As a result, a distinction was to be drawn between those grounds where no different treatment can be justified and other lesser forms of status which simply require some rational justification. Public interest concerns normally drive differences in these lesser forms of status and, as such, these are legitimate matters for government. Accordingly, such differences in treatment could be straight-forwardly rationally justified. In *Esfandiari and Others v Secretary of State for Work and Pensions* (2006), the Court of Appeal in England held that the rule in Britain that a funeral must take place in the UK to qualify for a Social Fund payment was not contrary to Article 14. The argument that the rule discriminated against recent migrants was rejected. In any event, the Court of Appeal ruled that any discrimination could be objectively justified.

An example of where Article 14 was successfully argued in a social security case was *Niedzwiecki v Germany* (2005). In Niedzwiecki, the applicant was a failed asylum seeker who had nonetheless been granted a provisional residence permit. He was refused child benefits on the basis that they were only granted to those likely to stay in Germany on a permanent basis and without an unlimited residence permit he did not fulfil the conditions of entitlement. The Court upheld his complaint, ruling that Article 8 was engaged as granting child benefits was a demonstration of respect for family life. While acknowledging that a government has a margin of appreciation in differential treatment there will be unlawful discrimination where there is not a reasonable relationship of proportionality between the means employed and the aim being realised. The Court went on to hold that there was no objective justification to treat migrants with a permanent resident permit differently from those with only a provisional permit when deciding who should be entitled to child benefits. This case is significant when considering the topical issue of differences in entitlement to social security benefits that apply to migrant workers and does not seem to have been argued in *Esfandiari*.

Article 15

RESERVATIONS & DEROGATIONS

1. In time of war or other public emergency threatening the life of the nation any Contracting Party may take measures derogating from its obligations under this Convention to the extent strictly required by the exigencies of the situation, provided that such measures are not inconsistent with other obligations under international law.

2. No derogation from Article 2, except in respect of deaths resulting from the lawful acts of war, or from Articles 3, 4 (paragraph 1) and shall be made under this provision.

3. Any High Contracting Party availing itself of this right of derogation shall keep the Secretary General of the Council of Europe fully informed of the measures which it has taken and the reasons therefor. It shall also inform the Secretary General of the Council of Europe when such measures have ceased to operate and the provisions of the Convention are again being fully executed.

Article 15 of the Convention allows derogations from the Convention in times of war and public emergency. Such derogations must be proportionate to this crisis and must not breach other international obligations. Under section 1(2) of the Act, any designated derogation will have effect in domestic law. Consequently, any amendment or end to a derogation will be reflected in domestic legislation. An initial derogation contained in Schedule 3 to the Act was withdrawn when the Terror Act 2000 came into force.

Any future derogations will be designated by an Order laid before Parliament under Article 14(4)(a) of the Act. Such an Order must be approved by both the House of Commons and House of Lords by a resolution within 40 days, otherwise it will cease to have any effect (except for the interim period). Under Section 16, designated derogations will cease to have effect after five years unless renewed.

The United Kingdom government has entered one reservation to the Convention under Article 64 of the Convention. This qualifies the right to education's respect for parents' philosophical and religious convictions in education and teaching so as to protect it only so far as is compatible with efficient instruction and training and avoidance of unreasonable public expenditure. See Article 2 of Protocol 1 Under the Act, this reservation and any future reservations will have effect in domestic law under Article 15 of the Act.

Unlike derogations, reservations are not subject to periodic renewal. The full text of the right to education reservation is contained in Part II of Schedule 3 of the Act.

Article 1, Protocol 1

THE RIGHT TO PROPERTY

Every natural or legal person is entitled to the peaceful enjoyment of his possessions. No one shall be deprived of his possessions except in the public interest and subject to the conditions provided for by law and by the general principles of international law. The preceding provisions shall not, however, in any way impair the right of a state to enforce such laws as it deems necessary to control the use of property in accordance with the general interest or to secure the payment of taxes or other contributions or penalties.

Article 1 of the Protocol 1 is often invoked, yet violations are rarely found because the permissible restrictions on the right are so widely drawn. However, the Court often finds a violation of an ancillary article, for example Article 6 or Article 8, where the interference is justified but not in the manner in which it has been carried out. In more recent times, the Court has made a number of landmark decisions, for example on social security benefits which have opened up the scope of Article 1 of the Protocol 1.

In effect, Article 1, Protocol 1 provides that a person has a right to peaceful enjoyment of property, that deprivation of property can only occur subject to specific conditions and that any interference by a government with the control of property must be in accordance with the general interest.

What is covered?

The term 'possessions' has been broadly inter-preted to include not only land but other interests with a financial value, for example, leases, patents, judgment debts, social security assistance and the exclusive hunting rights of indigenous peoples.

Social security benefits

With regard to paying contributions into a social security scheme, in *Muller v Austria* (1975), the Court held that this may, in certain circumstances, give rise to a property right over part of the assets contained in the scheme. Pension funds including private pension schemes are, therefore, likely to constitute possessions for the purposes of Article 1, Protocol 1. In *Carson and Reynolds v Secretary of State for Work and Pensions* (2003), the Court of Appeal in England upheld a ruling that Article 1 of Protocol 1 does not guarantee a pension of a particular amount, but merely a payment out of the fund. As a result, the freezing of the pension following emigration did not constitute a deprivation of a possession. The House of Lords in 2005 did not address the Article 1 of the Protocol 1 point, holding that even if the pension was a benefit there was no breach of Article 14 (freedom from discrimination).

In *Willis v UK* (2002), the Court held that a Widow's Payment and Widowed Mother's Allowance both came within the ambit of Article 1 of Protocol 1 even where Mr Willis was relying on his late wife's contributions to establish entitlement to benefit. The Court did not rule on the question of whether future entitlement to a Widow's Pension was covered by Article 1 of Protocol 1. The question whether entitlement to a Widow's Pension is covered by Article 1 was considered in the cases of *Runkee and White v UK* (2007) (see discussion in Article 14, freedom from discrimination).

In *Carson and Reynolds v Secretary of State for Work and Pensions* (2003), the High Court in England held that Income Support was not a possession for the purposes of Article 1 as the benefit has no link to contributions. In contrast, contributory Jobseeker's Allowance was held to be a possession though this did not confer a right to a particular level of benefit (ie the same rate of payment as that made to people aged 25 or older). The House of Lords in hearing this case alongside Carson again did not rule on this issue, holding that there was no breach of Article 14.

The Court has recently taken a much broader view of Article 1 and its application to social security benefits. In *Poirrez v France* (2003), the applicant was from the Ivory Coast and had been adopted by a French national when 21 years of age. The applicant had a severe disability from a young age but was refused a disability allowance on the grounds he was not a French national. Eventually, the nationality condition was lifted by a change in the law. The Court in dealing with the earlier period held there was no objective and reasonable justification for the difference in treatment and that the adult disabled living allowance was a possession for the purposes of Article 1. In *Stec v UK* (2005), the Grand Chamber of the Court in an admissibility ruling had to consider whether an industrial injuries benefit (Reduced Earnings Allowance) was a possession covered by Article 1. The Court held that given the variety of funding methods, and the interlocking nature of benefits under most welfare systems, it appears increasingly artificial to hold that only benefits financed by contributions to a specific fund fall within the scope of Article 1 of Protocol 1. Moreover, to exclude benefits paid for out of general taxation would be to disregard the fact that many claimants under this latter type of system also contribute to its financing through the payment of tax. This decision effectively ends the distinction between contributory and non-contributory benefits when deciding what falls within the scope of Article 1 of Protocol 1. The Court did go on to emphasise that the ruling does not restrict a contracting state's freedom to decide whether or not to put in place any form of social assistance scheme or to choose the level of benefit paid under any such scheme. However, once legislation is in place providing payment of a social security benefit as of right, then (regardless of whether based on contributions) this generates a proprietary interest falling within the reach of Article 1 of Protocol 1. The main issue before the Court was decided in *Stec v UK* (2006). The Court held that reduction in payments of Reduced Earnings Allowance at pensionable age (60

for women and 65 for men) was not contrary to Article 14.

An example of the importance of social security benefits falling within Article 1 of Protocol 1 is *Asmundsson v Iceland* (2004). In Asmundsson the applicant had been receiving a disability payment under a Seaman's Pension Fund following an accident at work. The eligibility criteria for payments were changed by the Icelandic government and the applicant lost his entitlement to payments after a five-year period offering protection against loss of entitlement had elapsed. The Court in hearing the challenge decided that the termination of the disability pension payment was an interference with the right to peaceful enjoyment of possessions. Further, the Court decided the Icelandic government had failed to strike a fair balance between the general interests of the community and the requirement to protect the individual's rights. The Court held that given the financial health of the fund the government could scale down payments. In this case, the method chosen left the applicant without any support from the fund and this was excessive, disproportionate and a fairer scheme should have been devised.

What is not covered?

In *FRG (Dec)* (1981) the right to a driving licence has been held not to be a possession. In Re *Chamber's application* (2005), the High Court in Northern Ireland held that the office of constable in the police service was not a possession for the purposes of Article 1 of Protocol 1. As a result, a challenge to a decision not to promote the applicant to the rank of sergeant was dismissed. In Re *McQuillan's application* (2004), the High Court in Northern Ireland was asked to consider whether the decision of a local council to pay a manual worker only half pay (rather than full pay) during a precautionary suspension was contrary to Article 1 Protocol 1, Article 14 and Article 8 of the Convention. The arrangement to pay only half pay was part of a negotiated collective agreement with a trade union. Other arrangements for non-manual workers allowed payment of full pay pending disciplinary proceedings. The High Court decided that the unpaid half pay was not a possession and, that even if it had been, the High Court would have found the interference was justified. Article 8 was also not engaged and therefore as Article 14 was not a free-standing right it could be examined. In *Nerva and others v UK* (2002), the Court held that tips in a customer's cheque or credit card payment were too imprecise to be treated as a possession. In this case, the national minimum wage was being paid and no right under Article 1 of Protocol 1 could be claimed to allow waiting staff to keep the additional sum.

Interferences with possessions

The Court has held that interference with possessions that are lawful include the suspension of an employee's pension permitted within an employment contract, a charging order on property in civil proceedings and the division of possessions as a result of a matrimonial dispute. The Court has held that the margin of appreciation to interfere with a property right is a wide one, although such interference must have a legitimate aim and must not be without foundation. Such interference must also be proportionate, with a fair balance being struck between the general interest of the community and the requirement to protect an individual's fundamental rights.

An example where this balance was not struck is Re *Landlords' Association for Northern Ireland and Others application for Judicial Review* (2005) in the High Court in Northern Ireland. The Landlords' Association successfully challenged a statutory scheme produced by the Housing Executive to register houses in multiple occupation. The High Court observed that any interference with the peaceful enjoyment of property must strike a balance between community and personal rights and the means adopted must be proportionate to the legitimate aim being pursued. The state has also to be given an appropriate margin of appreciation. Breach of the scheme devised by the Housing Executive constituted a criminal offence and must therefore be strictly interpreted and the scheme must be precise and clear. In this case the scheme was so vague and undefined in scope that its interference with property rights could not be justified.

Property cases

The Court has recently set out a number of key principles in *Kopecky v Slovakia* (2004) when dealing with Article 1 property cases. First, the Court said that Article 1 does not guarantee the right to acquire property. Second, any violation of Article 1 must relate to interference with peaceful enjoyment of possessions. Possessions can be either existing possessions or assets which a person can argue that he or she has a legitimate expectation of obtaining the effective enjoyment of, as a property right. Third, Article 1 cannot be interpreted as imposing any general obligation on contracting states to restore property transferred to the state before it ratified the Convention. In deciding how to deal with restitution of property the contracting state has a wide margin of appreciation to decide how restitution should be carried out.

The acceptance that there may be a property right based on a legitimate expectation of ownership is a development of the scope of Article 1 of Protocol 1. In *Stretch v UK* (2003), the Court applied the concept of legitimate expectation to a property right and applied Article 1. The applicant had leased land from a local authority for 22 years with an option to renew the lease for a further period. In accordance with the terms of the lease the applicant had developed the site. On renewal it became clear that the local authority had inadvertently acted unlawfully in agreeing the lease in the first place. As a result, the local authority refused to renew the agreement. The Court held this was a violation of Article 1.

A number of issues have arisen out of the compulsory purchase of land. In *Katikaridis and Others v Greece* (1996), the applicants' properties were bordering a main road and were compulsorily purchased by the local authority in order to provide road improvements. The compensation paid to the applicants was partially reduced as Greek law provided there was an irrefutable presumption that owners of adjoining properties derived a partial benefit from the new road. The Court held that this presumption was in violation of Article 1. In *Akkus v Turkey* (1997), the Court held that failure to pay compensation for seventeen months for compulsory purchase of land where inflation was at a rate of 70 per cent per year rendered the compensation inadequate and violated Article 1. In *Gaganus and Others v Turkey* (2001), the Court held that, in general, Article 1 required payment of compensation where property is compulsorily purchased in the public interest. In addition, the compensation should bear a reasonable relationship to the value of the property and payment should be made in a reasonably timely fashion.

A number of cases have also concerned the control of property. For example, in *Mellacher v Austria* (1989), a landlord challenged legislation to control rents. The Court, however, held that the legislation had a legitimate aim, namely to reduce excessive disparities between rents for equivalent properties and to combat property speculation. As a result, the Austrian government had not exceeded its wide margin of appreciation and there was no violation of Article 1. In *Palumbo (Eduardo) v Italy* (2000), the Court held that the applicant's inability to obtain possession of an apartment from a tenant for over seven years amounted to undue control of the use of property and a violation of Article 1. In *Hutten Czapska v Poland* (2006) the Grand Chamber considered an application arguing that laws restricting rent increases and termination of leases was contrary to Article 1. The Grand Chamber noted that the laws did not remove or transfer rights of ownership and the applicant retained a right to sell the property. Nonetheless, the statutory limitations imposed on the applicant did constitute a form of state control and could be covered by Article 1. The Grand Chamber observed that national authorities have a wide margin of appreciation in exercising control of property rights for policy reasons such as the protection of tenants' rights. In this case, the measures had a legitimate aim, however, the rent allowed was extremely low. As a result, the very essence of the applicant's right to property was impaired, namely the right to derive profit from the property. The disproportionate burden placed on the applicant could not be justified and a breach of Article 1 was accordingly upheld.

Finally, the Court has recently made an important decision in *J.A. Pye (Oxford) Ltd v UK* (2005). The applicant had permitted an individual to occupy fields for grazing. When the agreement ended, the applicant required the individual to leave the land. The land continued to be occupied and the applicant took no steps to regain the land. Fifteen years later after the death of the occupier of the land the applicant sought to regain the land against executors. The family members of the occupier claimed to have acquired the right to possession as a result of twelve years adverse possession under the Limitation Act 1980. The House of Lords upheld the rights of the family of the deceased occupier. The Court, however, overturned this decision and ruled that the Limitation Act deprived the applicant of the title to registered land and imposed an excessive burden. This burden upset the fair balance between the demands of public interest and the right of an individual to peaceful enjoyment of possessions, consequently there was a violation of Article 1. No decision was made on the question of compensation for the violation, which has been reserved until a later date. This case has been referred to the Grand Chamber of the Court and a further decision on this application will be issued in the near future.

Article 2, Protocol 1

THE RIGHT TO EDUCATION

No person shall be denied the right to education. In the exercise of any functions which it assumes in relation to education and to teaching, the state shall respect the right of parents to ensure such education and teaching in conformity with their own religious and philosophical convictions.

Article 2 guarantees the right to education, but does not oblige a government to provide this education. In effect, Article 2 is concerned with restricting government interference in education and requires a government to respect the right of parents to ensure that children are educated in line with the parents' religious and philosophical convictions. The UK government has entered a reservation in respect of this Article that:

in view of certain provisions of the Education Act in the United Kingdom, the principle affirmed *in the second sentence of Article 2 is accepted by the United Kingdom only insofar as it is compatible with efficient instruction and training and the avoidance of unreasonable public expenditure.*

Alhough Article 2 does not require a government to establish any specific education system, it does ensure that people living within that country shall have the right to avail themselves of the educational institutions provided. In *X v UK* (1978), parents complained that the failure to provide 100 per cent funding for integrated schools was a breach of Article 2. The application was held to be inadmissible.

In *Belgian Linguistic case (No 2)* (1968), the Court held there was no requirement that education should be available in any specific language other than that of the national language (or one of the national languages) of the contracting state.

Article 2 is primarily (but not exclusively) concerned with a right of access to primary rather than advanced or technical education: see *X v United Kingdom* (1978) unreported and *15 Foreign Students v United Kingdom* (1977). In *R (Douglas) v North Tyneside Metropolitan Borough Council and Secretary of State for Education and Skills* (2003), the Court of Appeal held that higher education was covered by Article 2. The case concerned the refusal of a student loan on grounds of age and the Court of Appeal held that failure to award a student loan did not violate a person's right to education. The Court has held that refusal to allow a child with a disability access to a normal school is not in breach of Article 2. Further, in *Belgian Linguistics (case No. 1)* (1967), the Court also held that the refusal of the Belgian authorities to establish or subsidise primary education in which French was the main language of education was not a violation of Article 2.

The Protocol does not prevent a government from making primary education compulsory. In addition, the Court has held that a government may regulate the right to education in accordance with needs and resources of the community and individuals. However, though there is a wide discretion in mak-

ing regulations, a government must abstain from any indoctrination which could offend a parent's religious or philosophical convictions. Article 2 of the Protocol provides, in effect, a right to respect for religious and philosophical convictions rather than an absolute right of a parent to have his or her child educated in accordance with religious and philosophical convictions.

In *Kjeldsen v Denmark* (1976), a number of parents complained about the imposition of compulsory sex education. The Court held that such education did not violate Article 2. In particular, it noted that a government is responsible for establishing a curriculum and this inevitably means that it will entail providing a direct or indirect philosophical approach through teaching or educational information or knowledge. If a general core curriculum were not allowable, then all forms of teaching would prove impracticable. However, the Court also noted that in fulfilling its functions with regard to education and teaching, a government must take care that information or knowledge included in the curriculum is conveyed in an objective, critical and pluralist manner. Further, a government is forbidden to pursue an aim of indoctrination that may be considered as not respecting a parent's religious and philosophical convictions. This is the limit which governments must not exceed.

A similar line was taken by the Court in *Alonso and Merino v Spain* (2000) where a mother complained about sex education classes. In this case, the lessons were held to consist of the imparting of objective information about sexual behaviour and not a form of indoctrination incompatible with the parents' religious and philosophical convictions. Furthermore, there was a large network of private schools and there was no obstacle to the parents enrolling their daughter in this alternative source of education. Article 2 of Protocol 1 did not confer a right to demand different lessons for a child in line with parents convictions.

In *W and DM v UK* (1984), parents challenged access to a single-sex grammar school because they had a fundamental objection to comprehensive education. The Commission ruled this did not amount to a philosophical conviction. Any challenge to a ban on academic selection on philosophical grounds is unlikely to succeed under Article 2.

In *Holub v Secretary of State for the Home Department* (2000), the Court of Appeal in England held that the right to education is not absolute and must be balanced against the interests of maintaining a fair immigration policy. The case concerned the decision to deport to Poland a child who was currently being educated in Britain. The Court of Appeal noted that the Secretary of State is expected to exercise discretion and take account of any educational difficulties created by a decision to deport when considering whether any compassionate grounds exist for granting leave to remain. However, the right to education in Article 2 is a right to an effective education of a minimum standard and whether the standard was as good as that available in Britain was not a material consideration.

In *Ali v Head Teachers and Governors of Lord Grey School* (2006) the House of Lords ruled that a young person removed from the school roll following allegations of setting fire to a classroom was not able to avail of Article 2. The House of Lords held that although the applicant had been unlawfully excluded this was due to a deficiency in statute law. Article 2 was held to guarantee fair and non-discriminatory access to the state education system; nonetheless, it provides no guarantee of a particular kind or quality of education or education at a particular institution. Expulsion from school does not breach the Convention unless and until there is no alternative stated education open to the child. It is important to remember, however, that Article 6 (the right to a fair trial) will be relevant to the conduct of disciplinary proceedings which may result in expulsion from school.

Article 3, Protocol 1

THE DUTY TO HOLD FREE ELECTIONS

The high contracting parties undertake to hold free elections at reasonable intervals by secret ballot under conditions which would ensure the free expression of the opinion of the people in the choice of the legislature.

The leading case on Article 3 of Protocol 1 is *Mathieu-Mochin and Clerfayt v Belgium* (1987). In this case, the Court said that free elections impose positive duties on a government and that the right to vote and the right to stand for election are protected rights. However, the Court went on to note that such rights are not absolute and can be subject to implied limitations as long as any such limitations do not interfere with the very essence of the right. In this case, the Court held that a regional council had sufficient competence and powers to be covered by Article 3. Elections to the Northern Ireland Assembly will therefore almost certainly be covered by Article 3 alongside Westminster elections and elections to the European Parliament: see *Matthews v UK* (1999) which establishes that the latter elections are covered. Other case law suggests that local council elections, referenda and appointment of a Head of State are all not covered by Article 3 (see Commission decisions *X v UK* (1972), *X v UK* (1975) and *Habsburg-Lothringen v Austria* (1989) respectively).

In *Ahmed and others v UK* (1998), examined earlier, the Court held that a prohibition on certain local government employees from campaigning and standing for election for a political party did not violate Article 3. The aim of the restriction was to maintain employees' political impartiality, which is an important aspect in the political system of the United Kingdom. The Court added that local government employees were free to resign from their jobs if they wished to stand for elections for the national or European Parliament.

When considering conditions imposed on the right to vote or to stand for election, the Court has held as reasonable residence conditions and restrictions preventing overseas nationals from voting; the provision of election deposits which are returnable only if a certain percentage of the vote is obtained; and the requirement of a minimum number of signatures for nomination to be obtained before a person can stand lawfully in an election.

In *Hirst v UK (No 2)* 2005, the Court sitting as a Grand Chamber held that the blanket ban on the right of convicted prisoners to vote was too widely drawn and a violation of Article 3. As a result of the judgment the government has agreed to amend the law on voting rights in prison.

Article 1, Protocol 6

ABOLITION OF THE DEATH PEN-ALTY

The death penalty shall be abolished. No one shall be condemned to such penalty or executed.

The effect of this provision is that the imposition of the death penalty will no longer be considered as a lawful exception to the prohibition on the deprivation to life in Article 2(1) of the Convention. No derogations are allowed under this Protocol.

It will be a violation of the Sixth Protocol for a state to sentence a person to death even where it has established a moratorium on the execution of the sentence. Moreover, once a state has abolished the death penalty, it is prohibited from re-introducing it, though governments are permitted to use the death penalty in times of war. Article 1 of Protocol 13 prohibits the death penalty absolutely, including in times of war and during imminent threat of war. The United Kingdom government has ratified both protocols.

A government may violate the Sixth Protocol if it extradites a person to a country where there is a real risk that the death penalty will be imposed.

Articles 1-5, Protocol 7

PROCEDURAL SAFEGUARDS RELATING TO THE EXPULSION OF ALIENS

This provision provides procedural rights and safeguards for those individuals who are lawfully living in a contracting state. The safeguards cover a right to submit reasons against expulsion, a right of review, a right to be represented and that any decision on expulsion must have been reached in accordance with the law. This protocol needs to be read alongside other parts of the Convention which have an effect on decisions on deportation, for example Article 3 (freedom from inhuman and degrading treatment) and Article 8 (right to family life).

Article 2 of the Protocol provides for a right of review or appeal against a criminal conviction or sentence. Article 3 ensures the right to compensation for miscarriages of justice. Article 4 gives the right not to be tried twice for the same criminal Act and Article 5 grants spouses equality of rights and responsibilities between each other and in relation to their children in private law proceedings. This Article does not fetter states from taking measures necessary in the interest of children.

THE HUMAN RIGHTS ACT

The Human Rights Act 1998 is a relatively short piece of legislation containing 22 sections and four schedules. It came into effect on 2 October 2000.

Section 1(1) sets out that the Convention rights protected by the Act are those contained in Articles 2 to 12 and 14, Articles 1 to 3 of the First Protocol and Article 1 of the Sixth Protocol as read with Articles 16 to 18 of the Convention. Article 16 provides for 'Restrictions on political activity of aliens' Article 17 that nothing in the Convention can be interpreted to imply that any state, group or person has the right to engage in activities or acts aimed at destroying or limiting rights and freedoms set out in the Convention; and Article 18 that limitations on rights and freedoms shall not be applied for any purpose beyond those prescribed within the Convention. Articles 1 and 13 are not included. These Articles cover the government's requirement to secure Convention rights to everyone within the jurisdiction and the right to an effective remedy respectively.

Arguably, the Human Rights Act goes only part of the way to meeting these requirements (creating only a declaration of incompatibility as the remedy to primary legislation which does not conform to the Convention stops short of meeting Article 1 and Article 13 in full).

For advisers, the Act has five key elements, namely:

- introducing a new rule of statutory interpretation whereby all legislation must be interpreted in a way that is compatible with the Convention wherever possible. Case law of the European Court (of Human Rights), European Commission and other rulings must be taken into account by courts, tribunals and other judicial bodies;

- providing courts and tribunals with new legal remedies so that, if legislation is not compatible with the Convention, then subordinate legislation can be struck down while primary legislation can be the subject of a declaration of incompatibility. This declaration does not invalidate the operation or prevent enforcement of legislation, but does mean that Parliament can look again at this legislation and fast-track amendments, if necessary;

- creating a duty on public authorities to operate in ways which are compatible with the Convention. The definition of public authority is widely drawn and includes courts and tribunals;

- strengthening remedies individuals have, in that a person who believes his or her Convention rights have been breached can take proceedings against a public authority or rely on Convention rights in proceedings taken against him or her by another party. Remedies available for a breach of Convention rights include damages, but only in courts already able to award damages (for example, this will not cover criminal courts or certain types of tribunals). A time limit of one year applies to bringing proceedings against a public authority though this can be extended at the discretion of the court or tribunal;

- ensuring that new legislation is proofed for its compatibility with the Convention. In Britain, a minister must make a statement of compatibility or state that he or she cannot make such a statement, but wishes to go ahead with the legislation in any event. In Northern Ireland, a minister must make a similar statement except that if an Assembly bill is not compatible, it cannot be introduced in that form.

The Human Rights Act covers the whole of the United Kingdom. The protections within the Act are augmented by the Northern Ireland Act 1998, which adds specific provisions governing legislation enacted by the Northern Ireland Assembly. The Northern Ireland Act introduced parts of the Human Rights Act from 2 December 1999 as regards the operation of the Northern Ireland Assembly and Executive.

INTERPRETING THE LAW AND THE EUROPEAN CONVENTION

Section 2 of the Act sets out that a court or tribunal determining a question on a Convention right must take into account where relevant to the proceedings any:

- judgment, decision, declaration or advisory opinion of the European Court of Human Rights;

- opinion of the Commission (as was) given in a report adopted by Article 31 (opinion on merits of the claims) of the Convention;

- decision of the Commission in connection with Article 26 or Article 27(2) (admissibility) of the Convention;

- decision of the Committee of Ministers taken under Article 46 of the Convention.

This section does not make the case law of the European Court binding on domestic courts and tribunals. Instead, such decisions must be taken into account and given proper credence. Case law to be considered is not confined to cases against the UK government. In arguing Convention case law, it is important to remember that a judgment of the European Court has greater weight than a European Commission decision, particularly on admissibility only, a decision of the Chamber of the Court has more authority than a decision of a Committee and a decision of the Grand Chamber has more authority than a decision of a Chamber.

Section 3 of the Act provides that, so far as it is possible to do so, primary and secondary legislation must be read and given effect in a way which is compatible with the rights contained in the Convention. The section applies to primary and secondary legislation enacted both before and after the introduction of the Act.

This section marks a sea change in statutory interpretation of the Convention. Prior to the Act, courts were only able to take the Convention into account where there was a clear ambiguity in legislation. Now a court or tribunal must interpret legislation to uphold Convention rights unless it is not possible to do so. By applying the Act to legislation introduced before as well as after October 2000, courts and tribunals will not automatically be bound by domestic case law if it is not itself compatible with Convention rights and case law. For example, a High Court may no longer have to automatically follow a judgment of the House of Lords if that judgment is not compatible with the Convention. Equally, a social security appeal tribunal may no longer be bound by a Northern Ireland Social Security Commissioner's decision in similar circumstances.

As the explanatory note to the Act sets out, the intention is to improve and supplement existing legal provisions safeguarding human rights law in the United Kingdom.

The Convention is an international treaty and is governed by rules of international law. Interpretation of international treaties is governed by the Vienna Convention on the Law of Treaties (1969). In particular, Article 31 of the Vienna Treaty provides that a treaty must be interpreted:

in good faith in accordance with the ordinary meaning to be given to the terms of the Treaty in their context and in light of its objects and purpose.

In effect, a purposive approach to interpreting the Convention has been adopted, ie to ensure its purpose is attained rather than strict construction of the wording of the Convention.

The European Court has also adopted an approach to the Convention that treats it as a living instrument which takes account of social developments and progress: for example, see *Tyrer v UK* (1981) on birching as a punishment, *Marckx v Belgium* (1980) on distinctions between legitimate and illegitimate children and *Goodwin v UK* (2002) on the rights of transsexuals.

In *Soering v UK* (1989), the Court neatly encapsulated the practical nature of interpreting the Convention.

in interpreting the Convention, regard must be had to its special character as a treaty for the collective enforcement of human rights and fundamental freedoms . . . Thus, the object and purpose of the Convention as an instrument for the protection of individual human beings require that its provisions be interpreted and applied so as to make its safeguards practical and effective.

All of this points to the need to give the Convention a wide and broad interpretation when considering its impact on domestic legislation. It also suggests that more contemporary decisions are likely to carry greater influence than older case law.

Domestic court cases have now provided an indication of how section 3 should work in practice. In *Poplar Housing and Regeneration Community Association Ltd v Donoghue* (2002), the Court of Appeal in England drew a distinction between interpretation and rewriting of legislation in applying section 3. In particular, the court noted:

It is difficult to overestimate the importance of section 3. It applies to legislation passed both before and after the Human Rights Act 1998 came into force. Subject to the section not requiring the court to go beyond what is possible, it is mandatory in its terms ... Now, when section 3 applies, the courts have to adjust their traditional role in relation to interpretation so as to give effect to the direction contained in section 3. It is as though legislation which predates the Human Rights Act 1998 and conflicts with the Convention has to be treated as being subsequently amended to incorporate the language of section. Section 3 does not entitle the court to legislate (its task is still one of interpretation, but interpretation in accordance with the direction contained in section) ...

The most difficult task which courts face is distinguishing between legislation and interpretation. Here practical experience of seeking to apply section 3 will provide the best guide. However, if it is necessary in order to obtain compliance to radically alter the effect of the legislation this will be an indication that more than interpretation is involved.

In *R v A (No 2)* 2002, the House of Lords considered section 3 when interpreting legislation governing evidence being given in rape trials. The House of Lords said that:

the interpretative obligation under section 3 is a strong one. It applies even if there is no ambiguity in the language in the sense of the language being capable of two different meanings. It is an emphatic adjuration by the legislature ... Section 3 places a duty on

the court to strive to find a possible interpretation compatible with Convention rights. Under ordinary methods of interpretation a court may depart from the language of the statute to avoid absurd consequences: section 3 goes much further ... Section 3 ... requires a court to find an interpretation compatible with Convention rights if it is possible to do so. In accordance with the will of Parliament as reflected in section 3 it will sometimes be necessary to adopt an interpretation which linguistically may appear strained. The techniques to be used will not only involve the reading down of express language in a statute but also the implication of provisions. A declaration of incompatibility is a measure of last resort. It must be avoided unless it is plainly impossible to do so.

The distinction between interpreting and re-writing legislation was also confirmed in the House of Lords in conjoined appeals *Re S (FC); Re S and Others; and Re W and Others (Children)* (2002) where it was stated that:

In applying section 3 courts must be ever mindful of this outer limit. The Human Rights Act reserves the amendment of primary legislation to Parliament. By this means the Act seeks to preserve parliamentary sovereignty. The Act maintains the constitutional boundary. Interpretation of statutes is a matter for the courts; the enactment of statutes, and the amendment of statutes, are matters for Parliament ... The area of real difficulty in identifying the limits of interpretation in a particular case ... For present purposes it is sufficient to say that a meaning which departs substantially from a fundamental feature of an Act of Parliament is likely to have crossed the boundary between interpretation and amendment. This is especially so where the departure has important practical repercussions which the court is not equipped to evaluate. In such a case the over-

all contextual setting may leave no scope for rendering the statutory provision Convention compliant by legitimate use of the process of interpretation.

As a result, the House of Lords overruled the Court of Appeal in England and Wales and held that the courts did not have powers to make interim care orders to supervise a local authority's treatment of children in its care. The Court of Appeal's interpretation had gone beyond the legislative innovation permitted by the Human Rights Act.

In *Ghaidan v Godin Mendoza* (2004), the House of Lords interpreted the Rent Act 1977 to ensure that the succession of private tenancies extended to same-sex couples. In doing so the House of Lords did not seek to rewrite or delete words from the legislation. Instead, the Law Lords indicated what they thought the substantive provision should achieve.

These decisions suggest that in approaching section 3 a court or tribunal should initially identify the legislative provision in breach of Convention rights. Where there is a breach, then section 3 should be examined to see if implying words into the legislation or a narrower interpretation can be applied to secure compatibility. This can be done without setting out the exact re-wording of the provision. This approach is subject to the limitation that if the re-interpretation conflicts with the clear expression of legislation or its necessary implication, or alters the statute in a fundamental way, then section 3 cannot be applied to provide a remedy. In *Hooper v Dept of Work and Pensions* (2002), the Court of Appeal in England and Wales issued a declaration of incompatibility against the failure to pay Widow's Payment and Widowed Mother's Allowance to widowers. The Court of Appeal held that the wording of the relevant legislation was unequivocal and clear and could not be subject to an alternative construction under section 3. The House of Lords went on to hear Hooper, though the declaration of incompatibility issued for failure to pay Widow's Payment and Widowed Mother's Allowance was not challenged.

The provisions contained in sections 2 and 3 make

it important that advisers are aware of Convention rights and case law.

NEW LEGAL REMEDIES FOR COURTS AND TRIBUNALS

Section 4 of the Act allows certain courts to issue a declaration of incompatibility between primary legislation and a Convention right. The section also provides courts and tribunals with powers to strike down subordinate legislation.

A declaration of incompatibility can be issued by the House of Lords, the Judicial Committee of the Privy Council, the Courts Martial Appeal Court, the Court of Session and High Court in Scotland (except where the latter is sitting other than as a trial court) and the High Court and Court of Appeal in England and Wales and Northern Ireland. Primary legislation is defined in section 21 and includes any public general Act, local and personal Act, any private Act (including an amending Act to public, general, private, local or personal Act) and an Order in Council made under certain legislation, including those made under the direct rule arrangements for Northern Ireland.

Where a court is considering the possibility of a declaration of incompatibility, the Crown has the right to be notified. This allows a minister to nominate a party or join the proceedings. In criminal proceedings where a minister has joined or nominated a party, then the minister or nominated party may seek leave to appeal to the House of Lords against any declaration of incompatibility.

A declaration of incompatibility neither binds the government to change legislation nor stops the legislation from continuing to operate. However, the government, in parliamentary debates and in the White Paper preceding the Act, made it clear that declarations of incompatibility will almost certainly lead to legislative change. In re *McR* (2002), the High Court in Northern Ireland declared that section 62 of the Offences Against the Person Act 1861 (dealing with buggery) was incompatible with Article 8 of the Convention as criminalisation of consensual acts was contrary to the right to private life. This matter was remedied by a change to sexual offences legislation in Northern Ireland. In *R (H) v Mental Health Review Tribunal North and East London Region* (2002), certain parts of the Mental Health Act 1983 were declared to be incompatible with Article 5 of the Convention and again the Act was then amended by Parliament.

With subordinate legislation, a court or tribunal can strike down or not apply a piece of legislation where it is impossible to interpret the legislation as being compatible with Convention rights. This is, in effect, a substantial extension of the *ultra vires* principle (ie that a public authority cannot act outside its powers). The court or tribunal may strike down or refuse to apply a specific part of subordinate legislation or the whole legislation. Subordinate legislation in section 21 is defined to include:

- Orders in Council except for those made in a way outlined in the definition of primary legislation in Northern Ireland;

- a measure of the Assembly established under Section 1 of the Northern Ireland Act 1973;

- an Act of the Northern Ireland Assembly;

- any order, rules, regulations, scheme, warrant, bylaw or other instrument made under primary legislation (except to the extent to which it operates to bring one or more provisions of that legislation into force or amends any primary legislation);

- any order, rules, regulations, scheme, warrant, bylaw or other instrument made by a Northern Ireland minister or Northern Ireland department, in exercise of royal prerogative or other executive functions of the Queen or which are exercisable by such a person on behalf of the Queen;

- any order, rules, regulations, scheme, warrant, bylaw or other instruments made under an Act of Parliament in Northern Ireland, a measure of the Assembly established under section 1 of the Northern Ireland Assembly Act 1973, an Act of the Northern Ireland Assembly or under an Order in Council applying only to Northern Ireland.

The wide definition of subordinate legislation means in effect that most legislation enacted in Northern Ireland will be treated as secondary legislation. For example, Health and Personal Social Services Orders are secondary legislation. Large swathes (though not all) of social security legislation will also be subordinate legislation. Most housing and employment legislation will also be subordinate legislation.

One important exception to a court or tribunal's power not to apply subordinate legislation which is incompatible with the Convention is where primary legislation prevents removal of the incompatibility (see section 3(2)(c) of the Act). In *R (Hooper) and others v Secretary of State for Work and Pensions* (2005), the House of Lords held that sections 6(2) (a) and (b) both precluded the Secretary of State from making extra-statutory payments to widowers to remedy any breach of the Convention for not making benefits available equivalent to those payable to widows. Once it was established the widowers were not covered by the primary legislation, payment on an extra-statutory basis (even if allowed under common law) would fall foul of both parts of section 6.

PUBLIC AUTHORITIES-NEW DUTIES

Section 6 of the Act requires public authorities to act in a way which is compatible with Convention rights unless acting in a different way is required to give effect to primary legislation (see reference to *Hooper* case above). This duty is not confined to a public authority's positive actions, but also covers a failure to take action. The duty does not extend, however, to include a failure to introduce legislation or a remedial order (another form of legislative provision designed to rectify incompatibility). 'Public authority' is defined in section 6(3) to specifically include courts and tribunals and any body, where some of its functions are of a public nature. The House of Commons and House of Lords are excluded from the definition, though the latter is covered in its role as a court.

Public bodies such as the Appeals Service and Central Office of Industrial Tribunals will be covered by section 6. Public authorities will also embrace government departments, non-departmental public bodies such as the Social Security Agency, Northern Ireland Housing Executive, health and social services boards and trusts (and their successors), local councils, Immigration Service and the police. A less clear-cut line will occur where a body carries out both public and private functions. A private security firm managing the transfer of immigration detainees to court and bail hearings will be a public authority when carrying out this task, but will not be covered when guarding commercial premises. Health service employees providing services within the NHS will be covered by section 6 for those functions, but not when maintaining private work separate from the health service.

In *Poplar Housing and Regeneration Community Association Ltd v Donoghue* (2002), the Court of Appeal in England held that the definition of what is a public authority and what is a public function should be given a generous interpretation. The Court of Appeal held that a housing association was so closely linked to a local authority that it was performing public rather than private functions. However, the decision also noted that the fact that a body performed functions which would otherwise have to be undertaken by a public body is not a conclusive factor. The County Court in Northern Ireland held, in *BIH Housing Association v Pavis* (2003) unreported, that a housing association was a public body for the purposes of the Human Rights Act.

In *R (Heather) v the Leonard Cheshire Foundation* (2002), the Court of Appeal held that the housing and residential care functions of the charity did not bring it within the definition of public authority even though it was publicly funded and regulated by the state and, in the absence of providing care, the state would have had to take its place. In the application of *YL v Birmingham City Council and others* (2007), a challenge was made in the Court of Appeal in England and Wales to the ruling in the Leonard Cheshire Foundation case. In this case the local authority had decided to transfer its residential care homes to the private sector. The applicants argued

that the transfer left the private body exercising public functions pursuant to the local authority's powers and duties. As a result, the Human Rights Act protections open to residents in local authority care should remain available. The Court of Appeal rejected the application, holding that it was bound by the decisions in *Donoghue and Leonard Cheshire Foundation*. This case was decided by the House of Lords who upheld by a majority the Court of Appeal decision. The government has announced its intention to amend the Human Rights Act.

In *Parochial Church Council of Parish of Aston Cantlow and Others v Wallbank* (2003), the House of Lords held that a parochial church council is not a core public authority within section 6. The Lords ruled that there is no single test for deciding whether a public function is being exercised. Instead there are a number of relevant factors which need to be taken into account. These include the extent to which the body receives public funding in carrying out its relevant function, whether statutory powers are being exercised and whether the authority is taking the place of central government or local authorities in undertaking its work or providing a public service. In *Aston Cantlow* the task being undertaken was the recovery of a civil debt and this did not fall within the relevant factors outlined above.

ENHANCED REMEDIES FOR INDIVIDUALS

Section 7 of the Act provides that a person may bring proceedings in a court or tribunal against a public authority which has acted (or proposes to act) in a way which is incompatible with Convention rights unless the public authority is required to act in this way to give effect to primary legislation. In addition, a person may rely on Convention rights in any legal proceedings. The time limit for bringing an action is tight. Section 7(5) sets out that a person must bring an action within a year of the act being complained of taking place or such longer period as a tribunal or court considers to be equitable in the circumstances. This is subject to any stricter time limit already in place for the procedure. As a result, the time for judicial review, namely, promptly and in any event within three months of the decision complained of, is not overridden by the Act.

There is no time limit governing the arguing of legal points in proceedings. This provision allows an individual to argue Convention legal points in criminal and civil proceedings or at appeals before a court or tribunal. The White Paper on the Act, *Bringing Rights Home*, suggests that this extends to arguing a point on Convention grounds alone where no domestic legal argument can be advanced. To exercise these rights, a person must be a victim as defined in section 7(7) of the Act which, in turn, refers to Article 34 of the Convention. Article 34 does not define the term victim, though it states that a person, non-governmental organisation or group of individuals who claim to be a victim of a violation by a government may apply to the court for a remedy. As a rule, the European Court has allowed actions to be taken by those directly affected by a particular act, although the applicant does not have to show that he or she has been subject to specific prejudice or detriment. In *Norris v Ireland* (1988) and *Dudgeon v UK* (1981), the fact that the risk of prosecution was nominal under legislation criminalising private acts between gay men did not prevent the applicant being treated as a victim of such legislation. In *Sutherland v UK* (2001), a challenge to the different age of consent for gay and heterosexual activity was settled after the government agreed to reduce the age of consent for gay acts for men to age sixteen through the Sexual (Offences) Amendment Act (2000).

The concept of victim also extends to family members, for example, following the death of an applicant. Non-governmental organisations, trade unions and professional associations can also take actions providing they can identify those directly affected by the action and show evidence of their authority to represent members. In judicial review proceedings, under section 7 a person is deemed to have a sufficient interest only if falling within the definition of victim. The question of who is a victim will almost certainly be the subject of litigation in its own right.

Section 8 sets out the powers of the court or tribunal where a public authority has acted (or proposes to act) unlawfully. Powers available include such relief, remedies and orders as are within the court's or tribunal's powers and are just and appropriate. This includes an award of damages where a court or tribunal has such powers or the quashing of a particular decision. If a court or tribunal has the general power to award damages then, under section 8(3), before such an award can be made, account must be taken of all the circumstances of the case including any other remedy granted and its consequence and whether a damages award will provide just satisfaction to the victim. Further, in deciding whether to make such an award and calculating damages, the domestic court or tribunal must take account of the principles applied by the European Court when awarding compensation under Article 41 of the Convention. The intention is to award compensation on an equivalent basis to that used by the European Court. The European Court awards compensation under three headings:

- pecuniary loss (ie actual loss such as lost earnings or pension rights);

- non-pecuniary loss (ie presumed loss such as anxiety, distress, feelings of injustice or lost employment opportunities); and

- costs and expenses incurred in taking legal action.

Interest is also payable on the above awards. The general aim of the Court is to put a person back in the position he or she would have been in but for the violation of a Convention right. In practice, working out the basis on which the Court awards compensation is not straightforward and the Court often holds that the declaration of a violation is itself a satisfactory remedy.

Special rules apply under section 9 where an individual claims that a judicial act has violated (or may violate) Convention rights. Any challenge can be brought only by exercising a right of appeal or through judicial review. Judicial acts include acts committed by judges, justices of the peace, court and tribunal clerks and tribunal members. No damages may be awarded against a judicial act done in good faith unless the issue concerns arrest or detention contrary to Article 5(5) of the Convention. In such cases, damages must be made against the Crown and the appropriate person (ie government minister or nominated representative) must be joined to the proceedings.

PROOFING NEW LEGISLATION

Section 19 of the Act requires ministers bringing forward new legislation to make a written statement that the legislation is compatible with Convention rights or that it is not compatible, but that the legislation will, nonetheless, proceed.

Under section 9 of the Northern Ireland Act 1998, a Northern Ireland minister must make a statement that a new Bill is compatible with the Convention. A provision of an Act which is incompatible with the Convention will be outside the legislative competence of the Assembly under section 6 of the Northern Ireland Act. This makes scrutiny of new legislation in light of the Convention particularly important.

TAKING CLAIMS BEFORE AND AFTER 2 OCTOBER 2000

No proceedings may be taken under the Human Rights Act against a public authority where the act or omission took place prior to 2 October 2000. However, this does not apply where proceedings are brought by or on behalf of a public authority where an act or omission can be challenged as incompatible with the Convention, even though the act or omission occurred before 2 October 2000. This provision is found in section 22(4) of the Act. In *R v Lambert* (2001), the House of Lords held that the Act does not generally apply retrospectively and appeals in relation to court or tribunal decisions made before 2 October 2000 cannot be made subject to the Human Rights Act.

This approach was more recently upheld by the House of Lords in *R (Hurst) v Chief Constable of the Metropolis* (2007) and *Jordan v Lord Chancellor* (2007) and *McCaughey v Chief Constable of Police Service NI* (2007) cases.

In Northern Ireland, Schedule 14 of the Northern Ireland Act 1998 has allowed any Acts of the Assembly, any subordinate legislation made by Northern Ireland departments and ministers and any act done by ministers and departments to be challenged as incompatible with the Convention from 2 December 1999. As a result, violations of the Convention before 2 October 2000 may be challenged if they are covered by Schedule 14.

CONCLUSION

This guide does no more than provide an overview of the European Convention on Human Rights and the Human Rights Act. Hopefully, it has illustrated the importance and potential of both pieces of legislation and whetted the appetite of the reader to find out more. Most legal disputes are resolved through negotiation and mediation and knowing whether and, if so, how the Convention and Human Rights Act apply is an important additional string to an adviser's bow. Moreover, there will continue to be issues of strategic public and legal importance which will come before the Court in Strasbourg and domestic courts. As the European Court interprets the Convention as an evolutionary document within signatory states, the Convention and the Human Rights Act will retain their contemporary importance.

FURTHER READING

European Human Rights Law: The Human Rights Act 1998 and European Convention on Human Rights, Keir Starmer, Legal Action Group, 242 Pentonville Road, London, N1 9UN (1999).

The Law of Human Rights, Richard Clayton and Hugh Tomlinson, Oxford University Press, Great Clarendon Street, Oxford, OX2 6DP (2000) (also publishes annual updates).

A Practitioner's Guide to the European Convention on Human Rights, 2nd edition, Karen Reid, Sweet and Maxwell, 100 Avenue Road, London, NW3 3PF (2004).

European Human Rights: Taking a case under the Convention, 2nd edition, Luke Clements, Nuala Mole and Alan Simmons, Sweet and Maxwell, 100 Avenue Road, Swiss Cottage, London, NW3 3PF(1999).

The Human Rights Act 1998: guidance for Northern Ireland Departments, Office of the First Minister and Deputy First Minister, Human Rights Directorate (2000).

European Human Rights Reports, published by Sweet and Maxwell, 100 Avenue Road, Swiss Cottage, London, NW3 3PF, available from Law Centre (NI) and Law Society libraries.

Taking a case to the European Court of Human Rights 2nd Edition, Philip Leach, Oxford University Press, Great Clarendon Street, Oxford (2005).

SOURCES OF ASSISTANCE

Law Centre (NI)

124 Donegall Street, Belfast, BT1 2GY. Telephone 028 9024 4401. Western Area Office: 9 Clarendon Street, Derry, BT48 7EP. Telephone 028 7126 2433.

Undertakes advice and casework referred by member agencies in employment, mental health, immigration, social security and community care including legal issues involving the Human Rights Act and European Convention.

The Northern Ireland Human Rights Commission

Temple Court, 39 North Street, Belfast, BT1 1NA. Telephone 028 9024 3987.

Provides advice on human rights issues and, in certain circumstances, will grant assistance to individuals.

The Committee on the Administration of Justice

45-47 Donegall Street, Belfast, BT1 2BR. Telephone 028 9096 1122.

Provides advice and assistance on human rights, legal issues covering criminal justice and certain civil justice issues.

Solicitors in private practice

Solicitors in private practice may take on cases for individuals relying, where appropriate, on the Legal Aid Scheme.

USEFUL WEBSITE & ADDRESSES

Court judgments are available from the Court's website at **www.echr.coe.int**

Published Court judgments can be obtained by subscribing to the *European Human Rights Reports* published by Sweet and Maxwell, 100 Avenue Road, Swiss Cottage, London, NW3 3PF.

Legal Action produces a twice-yearly update on European Court judgments in January and July, 242 Pentonville Road, London, N1 9UN.

Bulletin of Northern Ireland Law published by SLS Legal Publications (NI), provides details of Human Rights Act court judgments in Northern Ireland.

INDEX OF CASES